THE ULTIMATE INDONESIAN PHRASE BOOK

1001 INDONESIAN PHRASES FOR BEGINNERS AND BEYOND!

BY ADRIAN GEE

ISBN: 979-8-872064-05-3

Author's Note

Welcome to "The Ultimate Indonesian Phrase Book"! Embark on a captivating journey into the essence of Indonesian, a language known for its melodious rhythm and the rich cultural tapestry it weaves. Whether you're drawn to the majestic volcanoes of Java, the breathtaking beaches of Bali, or simply enchanted by Indonesia's diverse cultural heritage, this book is meticulously designed to make your language learning experience both immersive and rewarding.

As a fervent linguist and an enthusiast for cultural immersion, I appreciate the intricate process of language acquisition. This book is a product of that appreciation, crafted to be your faithful guide as you navigate the complexities of Indonesian language and culture.

Connect with Me: The adventure of learning a language goes beyond memorizing words and phrases—it's about forming connections and understanding the heart of a culture. I invite you to join me and fellow language enthusiasts on Instagram: @adriangruszka, a space thriving with the exchange of ideas and experiences.

Sharing is Caring: If this book becomes a key part of your journey in mastering Indonesian, I would be deeply honored by your recommendation to others who share our passion for the linguistic diversity of our planet. Feel free to share your learning milestones or moments of triumph on Instagram, and tag me – I'm excited to celebrate your progress!

Venturing into the Indonesian language is like exploring an archipelago of history, customs, and community spirit. Embrace the challenges, delight in your progress, and cherish every step of your Indonesian adventure.

Selamat belajar! (Happy learning!)

-Adrian Gee

CONTENTS

INTRODUCTION

Selamat datang! (Welcome!)

Whether you are fantasizing about a serene sunset on the shores of Bali, preparing to stroll through the bustling streets of Jakarta, seeking to engage with Indonesian speakers, or simply embracing the Indonesian language out of a love for its rich cultural background, this phrase book is crafted to be your reliable companion.

Embarking on the Indonesian language journey opens a door to a world marked by its vibrant diversity, rich cultural traditions, and a language that mirrors the archipelago's dynamic spirit and warmth.

Mengapa Bahasa Indonesia? (Why Indonesian?)

With over 270 million speakers, Indonesian is not just the language of the world's largest island country but also a central language in Southeast Asian communication, literature, and commerce. As the official language of Indonesia, it serves as a vital bridge for travelers, business people, and anyone enchanted by its rhythmic beauty and practicality.

Pengucapan (Pronunciation)

Before we dive into the vast collection of phrases and expressions, it's vital to acquaint yourself with the rhythmic flow of Indonesian. Each language has its own tempo and melody, and Indonesian is characterized by its fluid and gentle cadence, mirroring the welcoming nature of its people. Although its pronunciation may initially appear challenging, with dedication, the smooth syllables and harmonious tone patterns of Indonesian will become a delightful aspect of your language learning.

Indonesian pronunciation is noted for its clarity and consistency, with emphasis on open vowel sounds and gentle consonant articulation. The language's straightforward phonetic nature and lack of tonal variations make it accessible and enjoyable to learn. Mastering the pronunciation not only facilitates clear communication but also deepens your bond with the Indonesian people and their rich cultural heritage.

The Indonesian Alphabet

The Indonesian alphabet, like English, is based on the Latin script and consists of 26 letters. The pronunciation of these letters is generally more straightforward and consistent compared to English, making it easier for learners to grasp.

Vokal (Vowels)

A (a): Similar to the "a" in "father."
E (e): Pronounced like the "e" in "bed."
I (i): Similar to the "ee" in "see."
O (o): Like the "o" in "core," but more open.
U (u): Similar to the "oo" in "food."

Konsonan (Consonants)

B (b): As in English "bat."
C (c): Pronounced as "ch" in "chocolate."
D (d): Like the "d" in "dog."
F (f): As in English "far."
G (g): Like the "g" in "go."
H (h): Similar to the English "h" in "hat."
J (j): Like the "j" in "juice."
K (k): As in English "kite."

L (l): As in English "love."
M (m): Like the English "m" in "mother."
N (n): Like the "n" in "nice."
P (p): As in English "pen."
Q (q): Typically found in loanwords and pronounced like "k."
R (r): A rolling "r" pronounced at the front of the mouth.
S (s): Like the "s" in "see."
T (t): Like the "t" in "top."
V (v): Usually pronounced like "f" in Indonesian.
W (w): As in English "water."
X (x): Rarely used in Indonesian; typically in loanwords and pronounced like "ks."
Y (y): Similar to the "y" in "yes."
Z (z): Rare in Indonesian and usually found in loanwords; pronounced like the "z" in "zoo."

Note that the letters 'f', 'q', 'v', 'x', and 'z' are less commonly used in native Indonesian words and are more often seen in loanwords and foreign terms. Their pronunciation is usually influenced by the rules of the original language from which the word is borrowed.

Indonesian Intonation and Stress

Indonesian intonation is generally more level compared to the tonal languages of Southeast Asia, making it more accessible for non-native speakers. The key in Indonesian is clarity and rhythm. Emphasizing the correct syllable in a word is important as it often affects the meaning of the word.

Common Pronunciation Challenges

Kompleksitas Vokal (Vocal Complexities)

Indonesian vowels are generally straightforward, but the challenge lies in maintaining their purity without drifting into diphthongs, which are common in English. The difference in pronunciation of short and long vowels is subtle but crucial for clear communication.

Tips for Practicing Pronunciation

1. **Dengarkan dengan Saksama (Listen Attentively):** Engaging with Indonesian media, such as songs, podcasts, and films, is a great way to immerse yourself in the language's cadence and melody.

2. **Ulangi Setelah Penutur Asli (Repeat After a Native Speaker):** Practicing with a native speaker, either in person or via language learning apps, is crucial for refining your pronunciation.

3. **Gunakan Cermin (Use a Mirror):** Watching your mouth and facial expressions in a mirror can help you produce accurate Indonesian sounds.

4. **Latihan Secara Berkala (Practice Regularly):** Consistency in practice, even if it's just for a short time each day, is essential for improvement.

5. **Jangan Takut Salah (Don't Fear Mistakes):** Embrace errors as a natural part of the learning journey, leading to greater understanding and proficiency.

Mastering Indonesian pronunciation is essential to fully engage with its rich linguistic and cultural landscape. From the distinct clarity of its vowels to the rhythm of its syllables, each aspect of the language offers a glimpse into the diverse archipelago's heritage and traditions. With persistent practice and a keen ear for Indonesian's rhythmic nuances, your communication will not only convey your message but also reflect the warmth and hospitality inherent in Indonesian culture.

What You'll Find Inside

- **Frasa Penting (Essential Phrases):** A collection of carefully chosen phrases and expressions for various situations you might encounter in Indonesian-speaking contexts.

- **Latihan Interaktif (Interactive Exercises):** Engaging activities designed to test and improve your language skills, encouraging active use of Indonesian.

- **Wawasan Budaya (Cultural Insights):** Delve into the rich cultural landscape of Indonesian-speaking regions, from social customs to historical landmarks.

- **Sumber Tambahan (Additional Resources):** Recommendations for further materials and advice to deepen your Indonesian language skills, including websites, book suggestions, and travel tips.

How to Use This Phrase Book

This book is thoughtfully crafted to support beginners taking their initial steps into Indonesian, as well as intermediate learners looking to refine their skills. Begin your linguistic journey with essential phrases tailored for a variety of situations, from casual greetings to navigating the nuances of Indonesian social norms. As you grow more confident, explore more intricate language patterns and idiomatic expressions that bring you closer to the fluency of a native speaker.

Within these pages, you'll find cultural insights that create a deeper connection with Indonesia's rich history and vibrant contemporary life. Interactive exercises are interspersed throughout to reinforce your learning, helping you integrate new vocabulary and grammatical structures into your conversations with ease.

Learning a language is more than just memorization; it's an engaging and continuous pursuit of connection. Dive into Indonesian dialogues, explore the nation's diverse literary treasures, and acquaint yourself with customs that are integral to this unique culture.

Each person's journey towards language mastery is unique, characterized by its own pace and achievements. Nurture your skills with patience, enthusiasm, and an adventurous mindset. With consistent dedication, your proficiency and confidence in Indonesian will not just improve; they will flourish.

Siap untuk memulai? (Ready to start?)

Embark on an enriching exploration into the heart of the Indonesian language and culture. Unravel its linguistic intricacies and immerse yourself in the cultural richness that Indonesia offers. This journey promises to be as rewarding as it is transformative, expanding your horizons and enriching your global connections.

GREETINGS & INTRODUCTIONS

- BASIC GREETINGS -
- INTRODUCING YOURSELF AND OTHERS -
- EXPRESSING POLITENESS AND FORMALITY -

Basic Greetings

1. Hi!
   Hai!
   (Hah-ee!)

2. Hello!
   Halo!
   (Hah-loh!)

> **Idiomatic Expression:** "Bagai kacang lupa kulitnya." - Meaning: "To forget one's roots."
> (Literal Translation: "Like a peanut forgetting its shell.")

3. Good morning!
   Selamat pagi!
   (Se-lah-maht pah-gee!)

> **Cultural Insight:** Indonesian cuisine varies significantly between regions, reflecting the country's cultural diversity.

4. Good afternoon!
   Selamat siang!
   (Se-lah-maht see-ahng!)

5. Good evening!
   Selamat sore!
   (Se-lah-maht soh-reh!)

6. How are you?
   Apa kabar?
   (Ah-pah kah-bar?)

   Cultural Insight: Known for their warmth and politeness, Indonesians often use honorifics and polite forms in language.

7. Everything good?
   Semuanya baik?
   (Seh-moo-ahn-yah bah-ik?)

8. How is it going?
   Bagaimana kabarmu?
   (Bah-gah-ee-mah-nah kah-bar-moo?)

9. How is everything?
   Bagaimana semuanya?
   (Bah-gah-ee-mah-nah seh-moo-ahn-yah?)

10. I'm good, thank you.
    Saya baik, terima kasih.
    (Sah-yah bah-ik, teh-ree-mah kah-see.)

11. And you?
    Bagaimana dengan kamu?
    (Bah-gah-ee-mah-nah deh-ngahn kah-moo?)

12. Let me introduce...
    Izinkan saya memperkenalkan...
    (Ee-zin-kahn sah-yah mem-per-keh-nahl-kahn...)

13. This is...
    Ini adalah...
    (Ee-nee ah-dah-lah...)

14. Nice to meet you!
Senang bertemu dengan Anda!
(Seh-nahng ber-te-moo deh-ngahn Ahn-dah!)

15. Delighted!
Sangat senang!
(Sahng-aht seh-nahng!)

16. How have you been?
Bagaimana kabarmu?
(Bah-gah-ee-mah-nah kah-bar-moo?)

Politeness and Formality

17. Excuse me.
Permisi.
(Per-mee-see.)

18. Please.
Tolong.
(Toh-long.)

19. Thank you.
Terima kasih.
(Teh-ree-mah kah-see.)

Fun Fact: Indonesia consists of over 17,000 islands.

20. Thank you very much!
Terima kasih banyak!
(Teh-ree-mah kah-see bah-nyahk!)

21. I'm sorry.
    Maaf.
    (Mah-ahf.)

22. I apologize.
    Saya minta maaf.
    (Sah-yah meen-tah mah-ahf.)

23. Sir
    Tuan
    (Too-ahn)

24. Madam
    Nyonya
    (Nyo-nyah)

25. Miss
    Nona
    (No-nah)

26. Your name, please?
    Siapa nama Anda? (formal) / Siapa namamu? (informal)
    (See-ah-pah nah-mah Ahn-dah?) / (See-ah-pah nah-mah-moo?)

27. Can I help you with anything?
    Bisa saya bantu dengan sesuatu?
    (Bee-sah sah-yah bahn-too deh-ngahn seh-soo-ah-too?)

28. I am thankful for your help.
    Saya berterima kasih atas bantuan Anda.
    (Sah-yah ber-teh-ree-mah kah-see ah-tahs bahn-too-ahn Ahn-dah.)

29. The pleasure is mine.
    Senangnya milik saya.
    (Seh-nahng-nyah mee-leek sah-yah.)

30. Thank you for your hospitality.
Terima kasih atas keramahtamahan Anda.
(Teh-ree-mah kah-see ah-tahs keh-rah-mah-tah-mah-han Ahn-dah.)

31. It's nice to see you again.
Senang bertemu denganmu lagi.
(Seh-nahng ber-te-moo deh-ngahn-moo lah-gee.)

Greetings for Different Times of Day

32. Good morning, my friend!
Selamat pagi, temanku!
(Se-lah-maht pah-gee, teh-mahn-koo!)

33. Good afternoon, colleague!
Selamat siang, rekan kerja!
(Se-lah-maht see-ahng, reh-kahn kehr-jah!)

34. Good evening neighbor!
Selamat sore, tetangga!
(Se-lah-maht soh-reh, teh-tahng-gah!)

35. Have a good night!
Selamat malam!
(Se-lah-maht mah-lahm!)

36. Sleep well!
Tidur yang nyenyak!
(Tee-dur yahng nyeh-nyahk!)

Special Occasions

37. Happy birthday!
    Selamat ulang tahun!
    (Se-lah-maht oo-lahng tah-hoon!)

> **Language Learning Tip:** Practice Daily - Even a few minutes each day can make a significant difference.

38. Merry Christmas!
    Selamat Natal!
    (Se-lah-maht Nah-tahl!)

39. Happy Easter!
    Selamat Paskah!
    (Se-lah-maht Pahs-kah!)

> **Travel Story:** In the bustling streets of Jakarta, a local vendor, while haggling, used the phrase, "Ada harga, ada rupa," which translates to "There is a price, there is quality," highlighting the value for money.

40. Happy holidays!
    Selamat liburan!
    (Se-lah-maht lee-boo-rahn!)

41. Happy New Year!
    Selamat Tahun Baru!
    (Se-lah-maht Tah-hoon Bah-roo!)

> **Idiomatic Expression:** "Ada asap ada api." - Meaning: "Where there's smoke, there's fire." (Literal Translation: "Where there is smoke, there is fire.")

Meeting Someone for the First Time

42. Pleasure to meet you.
    Senang bertemu dengan Anda.
    (Seh-nahng ber-te-moo deh-ngahn Ahn-dah.)

> **Language Learning Tip:** Use Flashcards - They are great for memorizing vocabulary.

43. I am [Your Name].
    Nama saya [Nama Anda].
    (Nah-mah sah-yah [Nah-mah Ahn-dah].)

44. Where are you from?
    Dari mana asal Anda? (formal) / Dari mana asalmu? (informal)
    (Dah-ree mah-nah ah-sahl Ahn-dah?) / (Dah-ree mah-nah ah-sahl-moo?)

> **Language Learning Tip:** Listen to Indonesian Music - It helps with pronunciation and rhythm.

45. I'm on vacation.
    Saya sedang liburan.
    (Sah-yah seh-dahng lee-boo-rahn.)

46. What is your profession?
    Apa pekerjaan Anda? (formal) / Apa pekerjaanmu? (informal)
    (Ah-pah peh-kehr-jah-ahn Ahn-dah?) / (Ah-pah peh-kehr-jah-ahn-moo?)

47. How long will you stay here?
Anda akan tinggal di sini berapa lama?
(Ahn-dah ah-kahn teeng-gahl dee see-nee beh-rah-pah lah-mah?)

Responding to Greetings

48. Hello, how have you been?
Halo, apa kabar?
(Hah-loh, ah-pah kah-bar?)

Cultural Insight: Rice is not just a staple food but a cultural symbol, often associated with prosperity and life.

49. I've been very busy lately.
Akhir-akhir ini saya sangat sibuk.
(Ahk-heer ahk-heer ee-nee sah-yah sahng-aht see-book.)

50. I've had ups and downs.
Saya mengalami pasang surut.
(Sah-yah mehng-ah-lah-mee pah-sahng soo-root.)

Idiomatic Expression: "Bagai kucing dengan tikus." - Meaning: "Like cats and mice, often used to describe a situation of natural enemies."
Literal Translation: "Like a cat with a mouse."

51. Thanks for asking.
Terima kasih telah bertanya.
(Teh-ree-mah kah-see teh-lah ber-tahn-yah.)

52. I feel great.
Saya merasa sangat baik.
(Sah-yah meh-rah-sah sahng-aht bah-ik.)

53. Life has been good.
Hidup berjalan dengan baik.
(Hee-doop ber-jah-lahn deh-ngahn bah-ik.)

54. I can't complain.
Saya tidak bisa mengeluh.
(Sah-yah tee-dahk bee-sah mehng-eh-looh.)

55. And you, how are you?
Dan kamu, apa kabarmu?
(Dahn kah-moo, ah-pah kah-bar-moo?)

Language Learning Tip: Watch Indonesian Movies - With subtitles at first, then try without.

56. I've had some challenges.
Saya menghadapi beberapa tantangan.
(Sah-yah mehng-hah-dah-pee beh-beh-rah tahn-tahn-gahn.)

57. Life is a journey.
Hidup adalah sebuah perjalanan.
(Hee-doop ah-dah-lah seh-boo-ah per-jah-lah-nahn.)

58. Thank God, I'm fine.
Syukur, saya baik.
(Shoo-koor, sah-yah bah-ik.)

Informal Greetings

59. What's up?
    Ada apa?
    (Ah-dah ah-pah?)

60. All good?
    Semuanya baik?
    (Seh-moo-ahn-yah bah-ik?)

61. Hi, everything okay?
    Hai, semuanya baik-baik saja?
    (Hah-ee, seh-moo-ahn-yah bah-ik bah-ik sah-jah?)

62. I'm good, and you?
    Saya baik, dan kamu?
    (Sah-yah bah-ik, dahn kah-moo?)

63. How's life?
    Bagaimana kehidupanmu?
    (Bah-gah-ee-mah-nah keh-hee-doo-pahn-moo?)

64. Cool!
    Keren!
    (Keh-ren!)

Saying Goodbye

65. Goodbye!
    Selamat tinggal!
    (Seh-lah-maht teeng-gahl!)

66. See you later!
Sampai jumpa lagi!
(Sahm-pah-ee joom-pah lah-gee!)

> **Language Learning Tip:** Speak from Day One - Don't be afraid to start speaking Indonesian, even if it's just a few words or phrases.

67. Bye!
Selamat tinggal!
(Seh-lah-maht teeng-gahl!)

68. Have a good day.
Semoga hari Anda menyenangkan.
(Seh-moh-gah hah-ree Ahn-dah mehn-yen-ang-kahn.)

> **Language Learning Tip:** Record Yourself - Listen to your pronunciation and try to improve.

69. Have a good weekend.
Semoga akhir pekan Anda menyenangkan.
(Seh-moh-gah ahk-heer peh-kahn Ahn-dah mehn-yen-ang-kahn.)

70. Take care.
Jaga diri baik-baik.
(Jah-gah dee-ree bah-ik bah-ik.)

71. Bye, see you later.
Selamat tinggal, sampai jumpa lagi.
(Seh-lah-maht teeng-gahl, sahm-pah-ee joom-pah lah-gee.)

72. I need to go now.
Saya perlu pergi sekarang.
(Sah-yah pehr-loo pehr-gee seh-kah-rahng.)

73. Take care my friend!
    Jaga diri baik-baik, temanku!
    (Jah-gah dee-ree bah-ik bah-ik, teh-mahn-koo!)

Parting Words

74. Hope to see you soon.
    Semoga segera bertemu lagi.
    (Seh-moh-gah seh-geh-rah ber-te-moo lah-gee.)

75. Stay in touch.
    Tetap berhubungan.
    (Teh-tahp ber-hoo-boong-ahn.)

76. I'll miss you.
    Aku akan merindukanmu.
    (Ah-koo ah-kahn meh-rin-doo-kahn-moo.)

77. Be well.
    Semoga sehat selalu.
    (Seh-moh-gah seh-haht seh-lah-loo.)

"Bagai pinang dibelah dua."
"Like a betel nut split in two."
A perfect match or similarity between two things.

Interactive Challenge: Greetings Quiz

1. **How do you say "good morning" in Indonesian?**

   a) Apa yang kamu lakukan?
   b) Selamat pagi!
   c) Apa kabar?

2. **What does the Indonesian phrase "Senang bertemu dengan Anda" mean in English?**

   a) Excuse me!
   b) Pleased to meet you!
   c) How are you?

3. **When is it appropriate to use the phrase "Selamat malam!" in Indonesian?**

   a) In the morning
   b) In the afternoon
   c) In the evening

4. **Which phrase is used to ask someone how they are doing in Indonesian?**

   a) Terima kasih
   b) Apa kabar?
   c) Kemana kamu pergi?

5. **In Indonesia, when can you use the greeting "Halo!"?**

   a) Only in the morning
   b) Only in the afternoon
   c) Anytime

6. **What is the Indonesian equivalent of "And you?"?**

   a) Bagaimana dengan Anda?
   b) Terima kasih
   c) Apa yang kamu lakukan?

7. **When expressing gratitude in Indonesian, what do you say?**

   a) Maaf
   b) Senang bertemu dengan Anda
   c) Terima kasih

8. **How do you say "Excuse me" in Indonesian?**

   a) Permisi
   b) Selamat sore!
   c) Apakah semuanya baik?

9. **Which phrase is used to inquire about someone's well-being?**

   a) Di mana Anda tinggal?
   b) Apa kabar?
   c) Terima kasih

10. **In a typical Indonesian conversation, when is it common to ask about someone's background and interests during a first-time meeting?**

   a) Never
   b) Only in formal situations
   c) Always

11. In Indonesian, what does "Senang bertemu dengan Anda" mean?

a) Delighted to meet you
b) Excuse me
c) Thank you

12. When should you use the phrase "Apa kabar?"?

a) When ordering food
b) When asking for directions
c) When inquiring about someone's well-being

13. Which phrase is used to make requests politely?

a) Apa kabar?
b) Apa yang Anda inginkan?
c) Tolong

14. What is the equivalent of "I'm sorry" in Indonesian?

a) Maaf
b) Apa kabar?
c) Semuanya baik-baik saja

Correct Answers:

1. b)
2. b)
3. c)
4. b)
5. c)
6. a)
7. c)
8. a)
9. b)
10. c)
11. a)
12. c)
13. c)
14. a)

EATING & DINING

- ORDERING FOOD AND DRINKS IN A RESTAURANT -
- DIETARY PREFERENCES AND RESTRICTIONS -
- COMPLIMENTS AND COMPLAINTS ABOUT FOOD -

Basic Ordering

78. I'd like a table for two, please.
Tolong, saya ingin meja untuk dua orang.
(Toh-long, sah-yah een-geen meh-jah oon-took doo-ah oh-rahng.)

79. What's the special of the day?
Apa menu spesial hari ini?
(Ah-pah meh-noo speh-see-ahl hah-ree ee-nee?)

Cultural Insight: Unique to Bali, this form of Hinduism is a blend of local beliefs and Hindu influences.

80. Can I see the menu, please?
Bisa lihat menu, tolong?
(Bee-sah lee-haht meh-noo, toh-long?)

81. I'll have the steak, medium rare.
Saya pesan steak, setengah matang.
(Sah-yah peh-sahn steak, seh-tehng-ahh mah-tahng.)

82. Can I get a glass of water?
Bisa saya dapat segelas air, tolong?
(Bee-sah sah-yah dah-paht seh-geh-lahs ah-eer, toh-long?)

Travel Story: At the serene Borobudur Temple, a guide described the intricate carvings as "Seperti kacang lupa kulit," meaning "Like a peanut forgetting its shell," reflecting on how history can often forget its origins.

83. Can you bring us some bread to start?
Bisa bawa kami sedikit roti untuk permulaan?
(Bee-sah bah-wah kah-mee seh-dee-keet roh-tee oon-took pehr-moo-lahn?)

84. Do you have a vegetarian option?
Ada pilihan vegetarian?
(Ah-dah pee-lee-ahn veh-je-tah-ree-ahn?)

Language Learning Tip: Immerse Yourself - Surround yourself with the language as much as possible.

85. Is there a kids' menu available?
Ada menu anak-anak?
(Ah-dah meh-noo ah-nak ah-nak?)

86. We'd like to order appetizers to share.
Kami ingin memesan makanan pembuka untuk dibagi.
(Kah-mee een-geen meh-meh-sahn mah-kah-nahn pehm-boo-kah oon-took dee-bah-gee.)

87. Can we have separate checks, please?
Bisa kami mendapatkan tagihan terpisah, tolong?
(Bee-sah kah-mee mehn-dah-pah-tahn tah-gee-hahn tehr-pee-sahh, toh-long?)

88. Could you recommend a vegetarian dish?
Bisa merekomendasikan hidangan vegetarian?
(Bee-sah meh-reh-koh-men-dah-see-kahn hee-dahng-ahn veh-je-tah-ree-ahn?)

89. I'd like to try the local cuisine.
Saya ingin mencoba masakan lokal.
(Sah-yah een-geen men-cho-bah mah-sah-kahn loh-kahl.)

90. May I have a refill on my drink, please?
Bisa isi ulang minuman saya, tolong?
(Bee-sah ee-see oo-lahng mee-noo-mahn sah-yah, toh-long?)

> **Language Learning Tip:** Travel to Indonesia - If possible, visiting Indonesia can dramatically improve your language skills.

91. What's the chef's special today?
Apa spesial koki hari ini?
(Ah-pah speh-see-ahl koh-kee hah-ree ee-nee?)

92. Can you make it extra spicy?
Bisa buat lebih pedas?
(Bee-sah boo-aht leh-beeh peh-dahs?)

93. I'll have the chef's tasting menu.
Saya akan pesan menu cicipan koki.
(Sah-yah ah-kahn peh-sahn meh-noo chee-chee-pahn koh-kee.)

Special Requests

94. I'm allergic to nuts. Is this dish nut-free?
Saya alergi kacang. Apakah hidangan ini bebas kacang?
(Sah-yah ah-lehr-gee kah-chahng. Ah-pah-kah hee-dahng-ahn ee-nee beh-bahs kah-chahng?)

95. I'm on a gluten-free diet. What can I have?
Saya sedang diet bebas gluten. Apa yang bisa saya makan?
(Sah-yah seh-dahng dee-eht beh-bahs gloo-ten. Ah-pah yahng bee-sah sah-yah mah-kahn?)

96. Can you make it less spicy, please?
Bisa buat kurang pedas, tolong?
(Bee-sah boo-aht koo-rahng peh-dahs, toh-long?)

> **Idiomatic Expression:** "Membeli kucing dalam karung." - Meaning: "Buying something without inspecting it first." (Literal translation: "Buying a cat in a sack.")

97. Can you recommend a local specialty?
Bisa merekomendasikan spesialitas lokal?
(Bee-sah meh-reh-koh-men-dah-see-kahn speh-see-ah-lee-tahs loh-kahl?)

98. Could I have my salad without onions?
Bisa saya dapat salad tanpa bawang?
(Bee-sah sah-yah dah-paht sah-lahd tahn-pah bah-wahng?)

99. Are there any daily specials?
Ada spesial harian?
(Ah-dah speh-see-ahl hah-ree-ahn?)

> **Fun Fact:** The Komodo Island is the only place in the world to see the Komodo dragon in the wild.

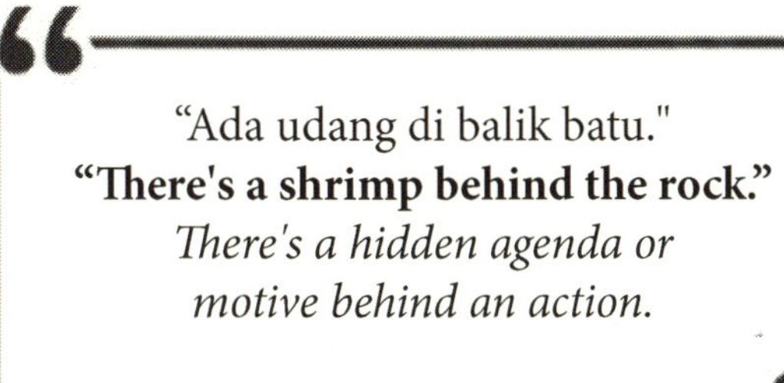

100. Can I get a side of extra sauce?
Bisa saya dapat saus tambahan?
(Bee-sah sah-yah dah-paht sah-oose tahm-bah-hahn?)

101. I'd like a glass of red/white wine, please.
Tolong, saya ingin segelas anggur merah/putih.
(Toh-long, sah-yah een-geen seh-geh-lahs ahng-goor meh-rah/poo-teeh.)

102. Could you bring the bill, please?
Bisa bawa tagihan, tolong?
(Bee-sah bah-wah tah-gee-hahn, toh-long?)

Allergies and Intolerances

103. I have a dairy allergy. Is the sauce dairy-free?
Saya alergi susu. Apakah saus ini bebas susu?
(Sah-yah ah-lehr-gee soo-soo. Ah-pah-kah sah-oose ee-nee beh-bahs soo-soo?)

> **Fun Fact:** Bali is famous for its beautiful beaches and is a top tourist destination.

104. Does this contain any seafood? I have an allergy.
Apakah makanan ini mengandung makanan laut? Saya punya alergi.
(Ah-pah-kah mah-kah-nahn ee-nee mehng-ahn-doong mah-kah-nahn lowt? Sah-yah poo-nyah ah-lehr-gee.)

105. I can't eat anything with soy. Is that an issue?
Saya tidak bisa makan apa pun dengan kedelai. Apakah itu masalah?
(Sah-yah tee-dahk bee-sah mah-kahn ah-pah poon deh-ngahn keh-deh-lie. Ah-pah-kah ee-too mah-sah-lah?)

106. I'm lactose intolerant, so no dairy, please.
Saya intoleran laktosa, jadi tolong tidak ada produk susu.
(Sah-yah een-toh-leh-rahn lahk-toh-sah, jah-dee toh-long tee-dahk ah-dah proh-duk soo-soo.)

107. Is there an option for those with nut allergies?
Apakah ada pilihan untuk orang yang alergi kacang?
(Ah-pah-kah ah-dah pee-lee-ahn oon-took oh-rahng yahng ah-lehr-gee kah-chahng?)

108. I'm following a vegan diet. Is that possible?
Saya mengikuti diet vegan. Apakah itu mungkin?
(Sah-yah mehng-ee-koo-tee dee-eht veh-gahn. Ah-pah-kah ee-too moo-mkin?)

> **Cultural Insight:** While Indonesia is predominantly Muslim, it officially recognizes six religions, reflecting religious diversity.

109. Is this dish suitable for someone with allergies?
Apakah hidangan ini cocok untuk orang dengan alergi?
(Ah-pah-kah hee-dahng-ahn ee-nee cho-chok oon-took oh-rahng deh-ngahn ah-lehr-gee?)

110. I'm trying to avoid dairy. Any dairy-free options?
Saya mencoba menghindari susu. Apakah ada pilihan bebas susu?
(Sah-yah mehn-cho-bah mehng-heen-dah-ree soo-soo. Ah-pah-kah ah-dah pee-lee-ahn beh-bahs soo-soo?)

111. I have a shellfish allergy. Is it safe to order seafood?
Saya alergi kerang. Apakah aman memesan makanan laut?
(Sah-yah ah-lehr-gee keh-rahng. Ah-pah-kah ah-mahn meh-meh-sahn mah-kah-nahn lowt?)

112. Can you make this gluten-free?
Bisa buat ini bebas gluten?
(Bee-sah boo-aht ee-nee beh-bahs gloo-ten?)

> **Language Learning Tip:** Use Indonesian Media - Read Indonesian newspapers or watch Indonesian news online.

Specific Dietary Requests

113. I prefer my food without cilantro.
Saya lebih suka makanan saya tanpa ketumbar.
(Sah-yah leh-beeh soo-kah mah-kah-nahn sah-yah tahn-pah keh-toom-bar.)

114. Could I have the dressing on the side?
Bisa saya dapatkan saus di samping?
(Bee-sah sah-yah dah-paht-kahn sah-oose dee sahm-ping?)

115. Can you make it vegan-friendly?
Bisa buat ini cocok untuk vegan?
(Bee-sah boo-aht ee-nee cho-chok oon-took veh-gahn?)

116. I'd like extra vegetables with my main course.
Saya ingin sayuran tambahan dengan makanan utama saya.
(Sah-yah een-geen sah-yoo-rahn tahm-bah-hahn deh-ngahn mah-kah-nahn oo-tah-mah sah-yah.)

117. Is this suitable for someone on a keto diet?
Apakah ini cocok untuk orang yang sedang diet keto?
(Ah-pah-kah ee-nee cho-chok oon-took oh-rahng yahng seh-dahng dee-eht keh-toh?)

118. I prefer my food with less oil, please.
Tolong, saya lebih suka makanan saya dengan minyak lebih sedikit.
(Toh-long, sah-yah leh-beeh soo-kah mah-kah-nahn sah-yah deh-ngahn meen-yahk leh-beeh seh-dee-keet.)

119. Is this dish suitable for vegetarians?
Apakah hidangan ini cocok untuk vejetarian?
(Ah-pah-kah hee-dahng-ahn ee-nee cho-chok oon-took veh-jeh-tah-ree-ahn?)

120. I'm on a low-carb diet. What would you recommend?
Saya sedang diet rendah karbohidrat. Apa yang Anda rekomendasikan?
(Sah-yah seh-dahng dee-eht rehn-dah kar-boh-hee-draht. Ah-pah yahng Ahn-dah reh-koh-men-dah-see-kahn?)

> **Fun Fact:** Indonesia's rainforests are among the world's most biologically diverse habitats.

121. Is the bread here gluten-free?
Apakah roti di sini bebas gluten?
(Ah-pah-kah roh-tee dee see-nee beh-bahs gloo-ten?)

122. I'm watching my sugar intake. Any sugar-free desserts?
Saya memperhatikan asupan gula saya. Ada dessert tanpa gula?
(Sah-yah mehm-pehr-hah-tee-kahn ah-soo-pahn goo-lah sah-yah. Ah-dah deh-sehr tahn-pah goo-lah?)

> **Travel Story:** In a vibrant market in Ubud, Bali, a craftsman selling colorful fabrics said, "Tak kenal maka tak sayang," implying "Not knowing, thus not loving," emphasizing the importance of understanding the culture behind the art.

Compliments

123. This meal is delicious!
Makanan ini sangat lezat!
(Mah-kah-nahn ee-nee sahng-aht leh-zat!)

> **Fun Fact:** Indonesia is part of the Coral Triangle, with the world's most diverse marine life.

124. The flavors in this dish are amazing.
Rasa dalam hidangan ini luar biasa.
(Rah-sah dah-lahm hee-dahng-ahn ee-nee loo-ar bee-ah-sah.)

125. I love the presentation of the food.
Saya suka penyajian makanannya.
(Sah-yah soo-kah peh-nyah-jee-ahn mah-kah-nahn-nyah.)

126. This dessert is outstanding!
Makanan penutup ini luar biasa!
(Mah-kah-nahn peh-noo-toop ee-nee loo-ar bee-ah-sah!)

127. The service here is exceptional.
Pelayanan di sini luar biasa.
(Peh-lah-yah-nahn dee see-nee loo-ar bee-ah-sah.)

> **Language Learning Tip:** Language Exchange - Find a language exchange partner or a tutor.

128. The chef deserves praise for this dish.
Koki pantas mendapat pujian untuk hidangan ini.
(Koh-kee pahn-tahs mehn-dah-paht poo-jee-ahn oon-took hee-dahng-ahn ee-nee.)

129. I'm impressed by the quality of the ingredients.
Saya terkesan dengan kualitas bahan-bahannya.
(Sah-yah tehr-keh-sahn deh-ngahn koo-ah-lee-tahs bah-han bah-hahn-nyah.)

130. The atmosphere in this restaurant is wonderful.
Suasana di restoran ini sangat menyenangkan.
(Soo-ah-sah-nah dee res-toh-rahn ee-nee sahng-aht mehn-yeh-nang-kahn.)

131. Everything we ordered was perfect.
Semua yang kami pesan sempurna.
(Seh-moo-ah yahng kah-mee peh-sahn sehm-poor-nah.)

Compaints

132. The food is cold. Can you reheat it?
Makanannya dingin. Bisa dipanaskan lagi?
(Mah-kah-nahn-nyah deen-geen. Bee-sah dee-pah-nahs-kahn lah-gee?)

> **Fun Fact:** The equator passes through 12 of Indonesia's islands.

133. This dish is too spicy for me.
Hidangan ini terlalu pedas untuk saya.
(Hee-dahng-ahn ee-nee tehr-lah-loo peh-dahs oon-took sah-yah.)

134. The portion size is quite small.
Ukuran porsinya cukup kecil.
(Oo-koo-rahn por-see-nyah coo-koop keh-cheel.)

135. There's a hair in my food.
Ada rambut di makanan saya.
(Ah-dah rahm-boot dee mah-kah-nahn sah-yah.)

136. I'm not satisfied with the service.
Saya tidak puas dengan layanannya.
(Sah-yah tee-dahk poo-ahs deh-ngahn lah-yahn-ahn-nyah.)

137. The soup is lukewarm.
Supnya hangat-hangat kuku.
(Soop-nyah hahng-aht-hahng-aht koo-koo.)

138. The sauce on this dish is too salty.
Saus di hidangan ini terlalu asin.
(Sah-oose dee hee-dahng-ahn ee-nee tehr-lah-loo ah-seen.)

> **Idiomatic Expression:** "Bagai pinang dibelah dua."
> Meaning: "Two of a kind."
> (Literal translation: "Like a betel nut split in two.")

139. The dessert was a bit disappointing.
Makanan penutup ini agak mengecewakan.
(Mah-kah-nahn peh-noo-toop ee-nee ah-gahk mehng-eh-cheh-wah-kahn.)

140. I ordered this dish, but you brought me something else.
Saya memesan hidangan ini, tapi Anda membawa sesuatu yang lain.
(Sah-yah meh-meh-sahn hee-dahng-ahn ee-nee, tah-pee Ahn-dah mehm-bah-wah seh-soo-ah-too yahng lie-n.)

141. The food took a long time to arrive.
Makanan lama datangnya.
(Mah-kah-nahn lah-mah dah-tahng-nyah.)

Specific Dish Feedback

142. The steak is overcooked.
Steaknya terlalu matang.
(Steh-ahk-nyah tehr-lah-loo mah-tahng.)

> **Fun Fact:** Over 3,000 traditional dances are recognized in Indonesia.

143. This pasta is undercooked.
Pasta ini kurang matang.
(Pah-stah ee-nee koo-rahng mah-tahng.)

144. The fish tastes off. Is it fresh?
Ikan ini rasanya aneh. Apakah segar?
(Ee-kahn ee-nee rah-sahn-yah ah-neh. Ah-pah-kah seh-gahr?)

145. The salad dressing is too sweet.
Saus salad ini terlalu manis.
(Sah-oose sah-lahd ee-nee tehr-lah-loo mah-nees.)

146. The rice is underseasoned.
Nasi ini kurang bumbu.
(Nah-see ee-nee koo-rahng boom-boo.)

> **Language Learning Tip:** Learn About Indonesian Culture - Understanding the culture helps in understanding the context of the language.

147. The dessert lacks flavor.
Makanan penutup ini kurang lezat.
(Mah-kah-nahn peh-noo-toop ee-nee koo-rahng leh-zat.)

148. The vegetables are overcooked.
Sayurannya terlalu matang.
(Sah-yoo-ran-nyah tehr-lah-loo mah-tahng.)

149. The pizza crust is burnt.
Kulit pizza terbakar.
(Koo-leet pee-zah tehr-bah-kahr.)

> **Travel Story:** On a scenic boat ride in Raja Ampat, a local fisherman mentioned "Bagai air di daun keladi," meaning "Like water on a taro leaf," when talking about the transient nature of life on the sea.

150. The burger is dry.
Burger ini kering.
(Boor-gher ee-nee keh-ring.)

151. The fries are too greasy.
Kentang gorengnya terlalu berminyak.
(Kehn-tahng goh-reng-nyah tehr-lah-loo berr-mee-nyahk.)

152. The soup is too watery.
Supnya terlalu encer.
(Soop-nyah tehr-lah-loo en-cher.)

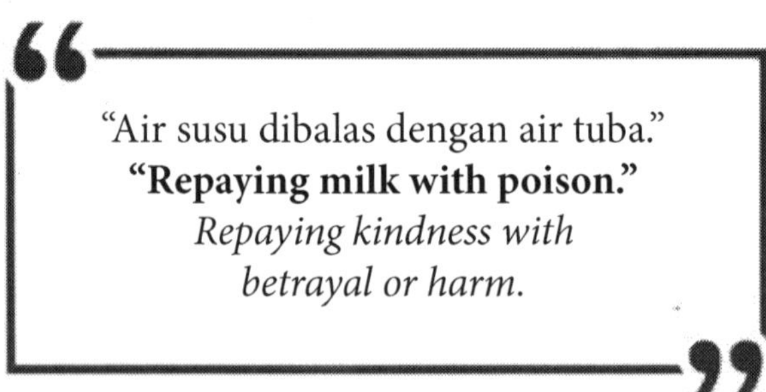

"Air susu dibalas dengan air tuba."
"Repaying milk with poison."
Repaying kindness with betrayal or harm.

Word Search Puzzle: Eating & Dining

RESTAURANT
RESTORAN
MENU
MENU
APPETIZER
HIDANGAN PEMBUKA
VEGETARIAN
VEGETARIAN
ALLERGY
ALERGI
VEGAN
VEGAN
SPECIAL
KHUSUS
DESSERT
HIDANGAN PENUTUP
SERVICE
LAYANAN
CHEF
KOKI
INGREDIENTS
BAHAN
ATMOSPHERE
SUASANA
PERFECT
SEMPURNA

```
A V E G A N T P C Z B H P D A
D P Y V B I E P D Q F I U E U
N G P A E M F E B S A D T C C
R A S E B G E O X P R A U N F
E K I U T C A T E E Q N N A Y
R T K R D I H N T C N G E D B
G A V F A D Z E E I A A P Y M
M U E X Y T W E F A R N Y L N
E F W H B T E Z R L O H E R U
I R V A O U N G S Y T A K N T
T R E S S E D A E G S U E V K
A K K H X C K U G V E M G X G
N E A W P H V T Q N R Y P S L
A T H Y U S C L A Y A N A N W
S U N S K E O J L M H D H E B
A I U A F Q Y M M E N U I A K
U S G R R S V X T D X V Y H O
S S E T F U W A A A I A G T K
P P N A I R A T E G E V R V I
N I V A C Y R T R K I E E D T
I L Z D Y G E E S N F V L T G
W R D W Y C L E G E L Q L L J
L F W C I A D R M K R X A M N
V J B V I C E N A H A B T S O
G U R M P D V K M H M M D K K
Z E U Q I V S L Q E X U S U G
S A X E L G E A Z S I L U X A
W Z N U J D C U K K Z Z F P I
U T F G W F Y L L M I A L R P
S E M P U R N A Q V W F I T B
```

Correct Answers:

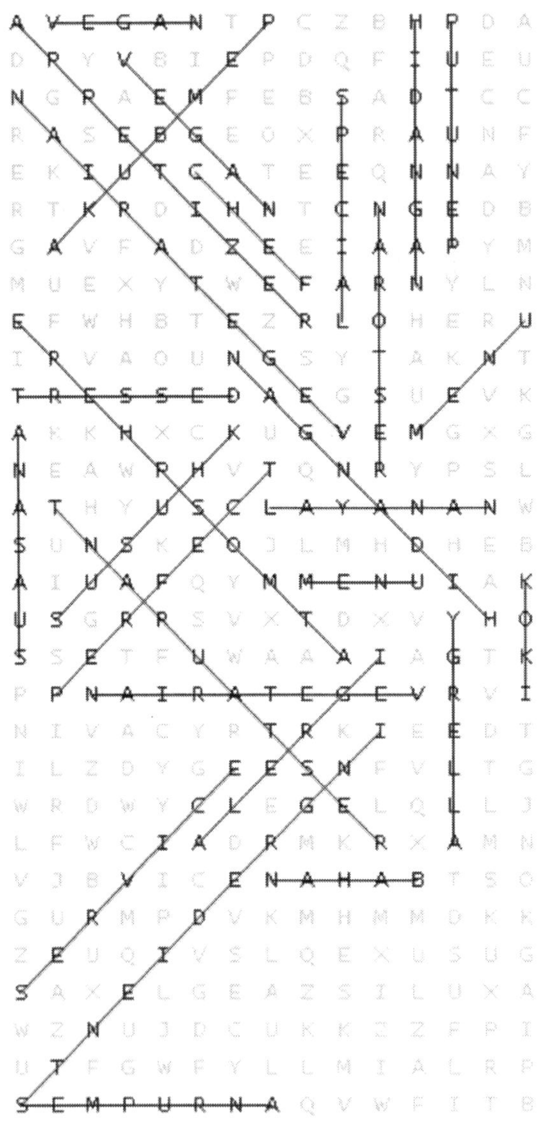

TRAVEL & TRANSPORTATION

- ASKING FOR DIRECTIONS -
- BUYING TICKETS FOR TRANSPORTATION -
- INQUIRING ABOUT TRAVEL-RELATED INFORMATION -

Directions

153. How do I get to the nearest bus stop?
Bagaimana cara saya ke halte bus terdekat?
(Bah-gah-ee-mah-nah chah-rah sah-yah keh hahl-teh boos tehr-deh-kat?)

> **Fun Fact:** The world's most populous island is Java, where Jakarta, the capital, is located.

154. Can you show me the way to the train station?
Bisakah Anda menunjukkan jalan ke stasiun kereta?
(Bee-sah-kah Ahn-dah meh-noon-jook-kahn jah-lahn keh stah-see-oon keh-reh-tah?)

155. Is there a map of the city center?
Apakah ada peta pusat kota?
(Ah-pah-kah ah-dah peh-tah poo-sat koh-tah?)

156. Which street leads to the airport?
Jalan mana yang menuju ke bandara?
(Jah-lahn mah-nah yahng meh-noo-joo keh bahn-dah-rah?)

157. Where is the nearest taxi stand?
Di mana halte taksi terdekat?
(Dee mah-nah hahl-teh tahk-see tehr-deh-kat?)

> **Travel Story:** In a Yogyakarta batik workshop, the artist explained the intricate process as "Sambil menyelam, minum air," literally "While diving, drink water," illustrating the art of multitasking.

158. How can I find the hotel from here?
Bagaimana saya menemukan hotel dari sini?
(Bah-gah-ee-mah-nah sah-yah meh-neh-moo-kahn ho-tel dah-ree see-nee?)

Fun Fact: Over 300 distinct native ethnicities are in Indonesia.

159. What's the quickest route to the museum?
Apa rute tercepat ke museum?
(Ah-pah roo-teh tehr-cheh-pat keh moo-seh-oom?)

160. Is there a pedestrian path to the beach?
Apakah ada jalur pejalan kaki ke pantai?
(Ah-pah-kah ah-dah jah-loor peh-jah-lahn kah-kee keh pahn-tie?)

161. Can you point me towards the city square?
Bisakah Anda mengarahkan saya ke alun-alun kota?
(Bee-sah-kah Ahn-dah mehng-ah-rahk-kahn sah-yah keh ah-loon ah-loon koh-tah?)

Idiomatic Expression: "Jatuh ke lubang yang sama." - Meaning: "To make the same mistake twice." (Literal translation: "Falling into the same hole.")

162. How do I find the trailhead for the hiking trail?
Bagaimana saya menemukan awal jalur pendakian?
(Bah-gah-ee-mah-nah sah-yah meh-neh-moo-kahn ah-wahl jah-loor pehn-dah-kee-ahn?)

Fun Fact: Indonesia is a leader in biodiesel production.

Ticket Purchase

163. How much is a one-way ticket to downtown?
Berapa harga tiket sekali jalan ke pusat kota?
(Beh-rah-pah hahr-gah tee-ket seh-kah-lee jah-lahn keh poo-saht koh-tah?)

164. Are there any discounts for students?
Apakah ada diskon untuk mahasiswa?
(Ah-pah-kah ah-dah dees-kohn oon-took mah-hah-swee-sah?)

> **Language Learning Tip:** Use Language Learning Apps - Apps like Duolingo, Babbel, or Rosetta Stone can be helpful.

165. What's the price of a monthly bus pass?
Berapa harga pas bulanan bus?
(Beh-rah-pah hahr-gah pahs boo-lah-nahn boos?)

166. Can I buy a metro ticket for a week?
Bisakah saya membeli tiket metro untuk satu minggu?
(Bee-sah-kah sah-yah mehm-beh-lee tee-ket meh-troh oon-took sah-too meeng-goo?)

167. How do I get a refund for a canceled flight?
Bagaimana saya mendapatkan pengembalian dana untuk penerbangan yang dibatalkan?
(Bah-gah-ee-mah-nah sah-yah mehn-dah-pah-tahn pehng-ehm-bah-lee-ahn dah-nah oon-took peh-ner-bahng-ahn yahng dee-bah-tahl-kahn?)

> **Fun Fact:** Indonesia has the world's largest Muslim population.

168. Is it cheaper to purchase tickets online or at the station?
Apakah lebih murah membeli tiket secara online atau di stasiun?
(Ah-pah-kah leh-beeh moo-rah mehm-beh-lee tee-ket seh-cah-rah ohn-lee-nay ah-tow dee stah-see-oon?)

169. Can I upgrade my bus ticket to first class?
Bisakah saya menaikkan kelas tiket bus saya ke kelas pertama?
(Bee-sah-kah sah-yah meh-nigh-kahn keh-lahs tee-ket boos sah-yah keh keh-lahs pehr-tah-mah?)

170. Are there any promotions for weekend train travel?
Apakah ada promosi untuk perjalanan kereta di akhir pekan?
(Ah-pah-kah ah-dah proh-moh-see oon-took pehr-jah-lah-nahn keh-reh-tah dee ahk-heer peh-kahn?)

171. Is there a night bus to the city center?
Apakah ada bus malam ke pusat kota?
(Ah-pah-kah ah-dah boos mah-lahm keh poo-saht koh-tah?)

> **Idiomatic Expression:** "Cuci mata." -
> Meaning: "Window shopping."
> (Literal translation: "Eye washing.")

172. What's the cost of a one-day tram pass?
Berapa harga tiket harian tram?
(Beh-rah-pah hahr-gah tee-ket hah-ree-ahn trahm?)

> **Fun Fact:** Indonesian has different levels of politeness in speech.

Travel Info

173. What's the weather forecast for tomorrow?
Bagaimana prakiraan cuaca untuk besok?
(Bah-gah-ee-mah-nah prah-kee-rahn choo-ah-chah oon-took beh-sohk?)

Fun Fact: Indonesian doesn't use articles like "a" or "the."

174. Are there any guided tours of the historical sites?
Apakah ada tur berpemandu di situs bersejarah?
(Ah-pah-kah ah-dah toor behr-peh-mahn-doo dee see-toos behr-seh-jah-rah?)

175. Can you recommend a good local restaurant for dinner?
Bisakah Anda merekomendasikan restoran lokal yang baik untuk makan malam?
(Bee-sah-kah Ahn-dah meh-reh-koh-men-dah-see-kahn res-toh-rahn loh-kahl yahng bah-ik oon-took mah-kahn mah-lahm?)

176. How do I get to the famous landmarks in town?
Bagaimana saya menuju ke landmark terkenal di kota?
(Bah-gah-ee-mah-nah sah-yah meh-noo-joo keh lehnd-mark tehr-keh-nahl dee koh-tah?)

177. Is there a visitor center at the airport?
Apakah di bandara ada pusat informasi pengunjung?
(Ah-pah-kah dee bahn-dah-rah ah-dah poo-saht een-for-mah-see pehng-oon-joong?)

178. What's the policy for bringing pets on the train?
Apa kebijakan membawa hewan peliharaan di kereta?
(Ah-pah keh-bee-jah-kahn mehm-bah-wah heh-wahn peh-lee-hah-rahn dee keh-reh-tah?)

179. Are there any discounts for disabled travelers?
Apakah ada diskon untuk para pelancong penyandang disabilitas?
(Ah-pah-kah ah-dah dees-kohn oon-took pah-rah peh-lahn-chong peh-nyahn-dahng dee-sah-bee-lee-tahs?)

> **Idiomatic Expression:** "Bak air di daun talas." - Meaning: "Something that does not last." (Literal translation: "Like water on a taro leaf.")

180. Can you provide information about local festivals?
Bisakah Anda memberikan informasi tentang festival lokal?
(Bee-sah-kah Ahn-dah mehm-beh-ree-kahn een-for-mah-see tehn-tahng fes-tee-val loh-kahl?)

181. Is there Wi-Fi available on long bus journeys?
Apakah ada Wi-Fi di perjalanan bus jarak jauh?
(Ah-pah-kah ah-dah wee-fee dee pehr-jah-lah-nahn boos jah-rahk jowh?)

> **Fun Fact:** Indonesia is a birdwatcher's paradise with numerous endemic species.

182. Where can I rent a bicycle for exploring the city?
Di mana saya bisa menyewa sepeda untuk menjelajahi kota?
(Dee mah-nah sah-yah bee-sah meh-nyeh-wah seh-peh-dah oon-took mehn-jeh-lah-hah-ee koh-tah?)

> **Travel Story:** On the sun-kissed beaches of Gili Islands, a fellow traveler described the sunset as "Seperti kacang lupa kulit," which means forgetting one's roots, as they felt lost in the beauty of nature.

Getting Around by Public Transportation

183. Which bus should I take to reach the city center?
Bus mana yang harus saya naiki untuk sampai ke pusat kota?
(Boos mah-nah yahng hah-roos sah-yah nah-ee-kee oon-took sahm-pie keh poo-saht koh-tah?)

184. Can I buy a day pass for unlimited rides?
Bisakah saya membeli tiket harian untuk perjalanan tak terbatas?
(Bee-sah-kah sah-yah mehm-beh-lee tee-ket hah-ree-ahn oon-took pehr-jah-lah-nahn tahk tehr-bah-tahs?)

185. Is there a metro station within walking distance?
Apakah ada stasiun metro yang bisa dijangkau dengan berjalan kaki?
(Ah-pah-kah ah-dah stah-see-oon meh-troh yahng bee-sah dee-jahng-kow deh-ngahn behr-jah-lahn kah-kee?)

186. How do I transfer between different bus lines?
Bagaimana cara berpindah antar jalur bus yang berbeda?
(Bah-gah-ee-mah-nah chah-rah behr-peen-dah ahn-tahr jah-loor boos yahng behr-beh-dah?)

187. Are there any discounts for senior citizens?
Apakah ada diskon untuk lansia?
(Ah-pah-kah ah-dah dees-kohn oon-took lahn-see-ah?)

188. What's the last bus/train for the night?
Bus/kereta apa yang terakhir untuk malam ini?
(Boos/keh-reh-tah ah-pah yahng tehr-ahk-heer oon-took mah-lahm ee-nee?)

189. Are there any express buses to [destination]?
Apakah ada bus ekspres ke [tujuan]?
(Ah-pah-kah ah-dah boos ek-spres keh [too-jooh-ahn]?)

"Sedia payung sebelum hujan."
"Prepare the umbrella before it rains."
Anticipate and prepare for potential problems.

190. Do trams run on weekends as well?
Apakah tram juga beroperasi di akhir pekan?
(Ah-pah-kah trahm joo-gah behr-oh-peh-rah-see dee ahk-heer peh-kahn?)

Fun Fact: Sumatra and Borneo are the only places in the world where orangutans are found in the wild.

191. Can you recommend a reliable taxi service?
Bisakah Anda merekomendasikan layanan taksi yang terpercaya?
(Bee-sah-kah Ahn-dah meh-reh-koh-men-dah-see-kahn lah-yah-nahn tahk-see yahng tehr-pehr-chah-yah?)

192. What's the fare for a one-way ticket to the suburbs?
Berapa tarif tiket sekali jalan ke pinggiran kota?
(Beh-rah-pah tah-reef tee-ket seh-kah-lee jah-lahn keh peeng-gee-ran koh-tah?)

Travel Story: At the historical site of Prambanan, a guide used the phrase "Air susu dibalas dengan air tuba," or "Repaying milk with poison," to describe the historical betrayals of kings.

Navigating the Airport

193. Where can I locate the baggage claim area?
Di mana saya bisa menemukan area pengambilan bagasi?
(Dee mah-nah sah-yah bee-sah meh-neh-moo-kahn ah-re-ah peh-ngahm-bee-lahn bah-gah-see?)

194. Is there a currency exchange counter in the terminal?
Apakah ada konter penukaran mata uang di terminal?
(Ah-pah-kah ah-dah kohn-tehr peh-noo-kah-rahn mah-tah oo-ahng dee ter-mee-nahl?)

> **Idiomatic Expression:** "Membuang muka." - Meaning: "To avoid someone."
> (Literal translation: "Throwing away the face.")

195. Are there any pet relief areas for service animals?
Apakah ada area khusus untuk hewan layanan?
(Ah-pah-kah ah-dah ah-re-ah koo-soos oon-took heh-wahn lah-yah-nahn?)

196. How early can I go through security?
Seberapa cepat saya bisa melewati keamanan?
(Seh-behr-pah cheh-paht sah-yah bee-sah meh-leh-wah-tee keh-ah-mah-nahn?)

197. What's the procedure for boarding the aircraft?
Apa prosedur untuk naik ke pesawat?
(Ah-pah proh-seh-door oon-took nah-ik keh peh-sah-waht?)

198. Can I use mobile boarding passes?
Bisakah saya menggunakan boarding pass mobile?
(Bee-sah-kah sah-yah mehng-goo-nah-kahn bohr-deeng pahs moh-beel?)

199. Are there any restaurants past security?
Apakah ada restoran setelah keamanan?
(Ah-pah-kah ah-dah res-toh-rahn seh-teh-lah keh-ah-mah-nahn?)

200. What's the airport's Wi-Fi password?
Apa kata sandi Wi-Fi di bandara?
(Ah-pah kah-tah sahn-dee Wee-Fee dee bahn-dah-rah?)

201. Can I bring duty-free items on board?
Bisakah saya membawa barang bebas pajak ke dalam pesawat?
(Bee-sah-kah sah-yah mehm-bah-wah bahr-ahng beh-bahs pah-jahk keh dah-lahm peh-sah-waht?)

202. Is there a pharmacy at the airport?
Apakah di bandara ada apotek?
(Ah-pah-kah dee bahn-dah-rah ah-dah ah-poh-tek?)

Traveling by Car

203. How do I pay tolls on the highway?
Bagaimana saya membayar tol di jalan tol?
(Bah-gah-ee-mah-nah sah-yah mehm-bah-yahr tohl dee jah-lahn tohl?)

204. Where can I find a car wash nearby?
Di mana saya bisa menemukan tempat cuci mobil terdekat?
(Dee mah-nah sah-yah bee-sah meh-neh-moo-kahn tehm-paht choo-chee moh-beel tehr-deh-kaht?)

205. Are there electric vehicle charging stations?
Apakah ada stasiun pengisian kendaraan listrik?
(Ah-pah-kah ah-dah stah-see-oon pehng-ee-see-ahn kehn-dah-rahn lees-treek?)

206. Can I rent a GPS navigation system with the car?
Bisakah saya menyewa sistem navigasi GPS bersama mobilnya?
(Bee-sah-kah sah-yah meh-nye-wah see-stehm nah-vee-gah-see Jee-Pee-Ess behr-sah-mah moh-beel-nyah?)

207. What's the cost of parking in the city center?
Berapa biaya parkir di pusat kota?
(Beh-rah-pah bee-ah-yah pahr-keer dee poo-saht koh-tah?)

208. Do I need an international driving permit?
Apakah saya memerlukan SIM Internasional?
(Ah-pah-kah sah-yah meh-mehr-loo-kahn SEEM Een-ter-nah-see-oh-nahl?)

209. Is roadside assistance available?
Apakah ada layanan bantuan di pinggir jalan?
(Ah-pah-kah ah-dah lah-yah-nahn bahn-too-ahn dee peeng-geer jah-lahn?)

210. Are there any traffic cameras on this route?
Apakah ada kamera lalu lintas di rute ini?
(Ah-pah-kah ah-dah kah-meh-rah lah-loo leen-tahs dee roo-teh ee-nee?)

211. Can you recommend a reliable mechanic?
Bisakah Anda merekomendasikan mekanik yang terpercaya?
(Bee-sah-kah Ahn-dah meh-reh-koh-men-dah-see-kahn meh-kah-neek yahng tehr-pehr-chah-yah?)

212. What's the speed limit in residential areas?
Berapa batas kecepatan di area perumahan?
(Beh-rah-pah bah-tahs keh-cheh-pah-tahn dee ah-re-ah peh-roo-mah-hahn?)

Airport Transfers and Shuttles

213. Where is the taxi stand located at the airport?
Di mana lokasi pangkalan taksi di bandara?
(Dee mah-nah loh-kah-see pahng-kah-lahn tak-see dee bahn-dah-rah?)

214. Do airport shuttles run 24/7?
Apakah shuttle bandara beroperasi 24 jam setiap hari?
(Ah-pah-kah shuht-tle bahn-dah-rah behr-oh-peh-rah-see doo-ah pooh-luh jam seh-tee-ahp hah-ree?)

Idiomatic Expression: "Mendapat durian runtuh." - Meaning: "An unexpected windfall." (Literal translation: "Getting a falling durian.")

215. How long does it take to reach downtown by taxi?
Berapa lama waktu yang diperlukan untuk sampai ke pusat kota dengan taksi?
(Beh-rah-pah lah-mah wahk-too yahng dee-pehr-loo-kahn oon-took sahm-pie keh poo-saht koh-tah dehng-ahn tak-see?)

216. Is there a designated pick-up area for ride-sharing services?
Apakah ada area khusus penjemputan untuk layanan berbagi tumpangan?
(Ah-pah-kah ah-dah ah-re-ah koo-soos pehn-jehm-poo-tahn oon-took lah-yah-nahn behr-bah-ghee toom-pahng-ahn?)

217. Can I book a shuttle in advance?
Bisakah saya memesan shuttle terlebih dahulu?
(Bee-sah-kah sah-yah meh-meh-sahn shuht-tle tehr-leh-beeh dah-hoo-loo?)

Fun Fact: Borobudur Temple is the world's largest Buddhist archaeological site.

218. Do hotels offer free shuttle service to the airport?
Apakah hotel menawarkan layanan shuttle gratis ke bandara?
(Ah-pah-kah ho-tel meh-nah-wahr-kahn lah-yah-nahn shuht-tle grah-tees keh bahn-dah-rah?)

219. What's the rate for a private airport transfer?
Berapa tarif untuk transfer bandara pribadi?
(Beh-rah-pah tah-reef oon-took trahns-fur bahn-dah-rah pree-bah-dee?)

220. Are there any public buses connecting to the airport?
Apakah ada bus umum yang menuju ke bandara?
(Ah-pah-kah ah-dah boos oo-moom yahng meh-noo-joo keh bahn-dah-rah?)

221. Can you recommend a reliable limousine service?
Bisakah Anda merekomendasikan layanan limusin yang terpercaya?
(Bee-sah-kah Ahn-dah meh-reh-koh-men-dah-see-kahn lah-yah-nahn lee-moo-seen yahng tehr-pehr-chah-yah?)

222. Is there an airport shuttle for early morning flights?
Apakah ada shuttle bandara untuk penerbangan pagi hari?
(Ah-pah-kah ah-dah shuht-tle bahn-dah-rah oon-took peh-ner-bahng-ahn pah-gee hah-ree?)

Traveling with Luggage

223. Can I check my bags at this train station?
Bisakah saya mengecek tas saya di stasiun kereta ini?
(Bee-sah-kah sah-yah mehn-geh-cek tahs sah-yah dee stah-see-oon keh-reh-tah ee-nee?)

224. Where can I find baggage carts in the airport?
Di mana saya bisa menemukan troli bagasi di bandara?
(Dee mah-nah sah-yah bee-sah meh-neh-moo-kahn troh-lee bah-gah-see dee bahn-dah-rah?)

> **Fun Fact:** Sumatran Tigers are found exclusively on the island of Sumatra.

225. Are there weight limits for checked baggage?
Apakah ada batasan berat untuk bagasi yang diperiksa?
(Ah-pah-kah ah-dah bah-tah-sahn beh-rah oon-took bah-gah-see yahng dee-peh-reek-sah?)

226. Can I carry my backpack as a personal item?
Bisakah saya membawa ransel sebagai barang pribadi?
(Bee-sah-kah sah-yah mehm-bah-wah rahn-sel seh-bah-guy bah-rang pree-bah-dee?)

227. What's the procedure for oversized luggage?
Apa prosedur untuk bagasi berukuran besar?
(Ah-pah proh-seh-door oon-took bah-gah-see beh-roo-koo-rahn beh-sahr?)

228. Can I bring a stroller on the bus?
Bisakah saya membawa stroller ke dalam bus?
(Bee-sah-kah sah-yah mehm-bah-wah strohl-ler keh dah-lahm boos?)

229. Are there lockers for storing luggage at the airport?
Apakah di bandara ada loker untuk menyimpan bagasi?
(Ah-pah-kah dee bahn-dah-rah ah-dah loh-ker oon-took meh-nee-sim-pahn bah-gah-see?)

> **Fun Fact:** Indonesian has no gender, no plurals, and no tenses, making its grammar relatively simple.

230. How do I label my luggage with contact information?
Bagaimana saya memberi label bagasi saya dengan informasi kontak?
(Bah-gah-ee-mah-nah sah-yah mehm-beh-ree lay-bel bah-gah-see sah-yah deh-ngahn een-for-mah-see kohn-tahk?)

231. Is there a lost and found office at the train station?
Apakah di stasiun kereta ada kantor barang hilang dan ditemukan?
(Ah-pah-kah dee stah-see-oon keh-reh-tah ah-dah kahn-tor bah-rahng hee-lahng dahn dee-teh-moo-kahn?)

> **Idiomatic Expression:** "Kacang lupa kulitnya." - Meaning: "Forget one's origins."
> (Literal translation: "A peanut forgets its skin.")

232. Can I carry fragile items in my checked bags?
Bisakah saya membawa barang-barang rapuh di dalam bagasi yang saya serahkan?
(Bee-sah-kah sah-yah mehm-bah-wah bah-rahng bah-rahng rah-puh dee dah-lahm bah-gah-see yahng sah-yah sehr-ah-hahn?)

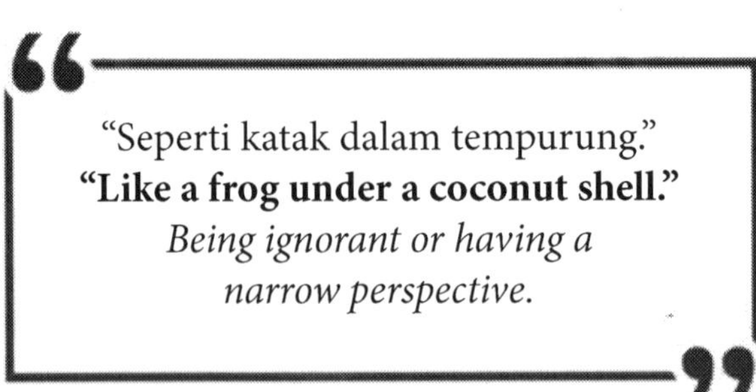

Word Search Puzzle: Travel & Transportation

AIRPORT
BANDARA
BUS
BUS
TAXI
TAKSI
TICKET
TIKET
MAP
PETA
CAR
MOBIL
METRO
METRO
BICYCLE
SEPEDA
DEPARTURE
KEBERANGKATAN
ARRIVAL
KEDATANGAN
ROAD
JALAN
PLATFORM
PERON
STATION
STASIUN
TERMINAL
TERMINAL

```
E R U T R A P E D J N A H O V
O Q Z Q C Q X W R V A V E D T
F F W M P F T B V D N L K B N
Y I R S Z K I T N Z I F A A M
V A P S P V C P G B V B G N J
J J T I N F K W O H I N S D E
H C Q E P U E M U J A E A H F
W W D L P B T C N T P W Y R W
Y W T R O P R I A E H Z L A Y
N O I T A T S D D F C K Z C Y
N S H R S P E A U B R G Z I Q
G A D Y E K S U R I I P G D S
F J T R O A D A I C L L F U A
H T O A C Y C S J Y A A B S L
K N Q G K N U T R C N T D E X
M E T R O G P A M L I F N W P
N X I M F T N T W E M O A D H
J U X R I K W A U M R R C M Z
J W I N I E Y V R T E M H T U
O Y I S N T W L K E T T I P E
R S E D A P A R B N B K R V L
A T E F M T A K L F E E I O A
A R Y L J D S F S T C M K L V
E R A S T A X I Z I W E A Q I
I O M D K V E I U A A N Q O R
N B W M N N I V I P I P Z V R
I T K F Y A A D N M B Y E X A
F R I T W S B T R Q P V E B Q
I C O L I U Q E I Z T E E W V
P N A F R B T K U A J Q J Z N
```

Correct Answers:

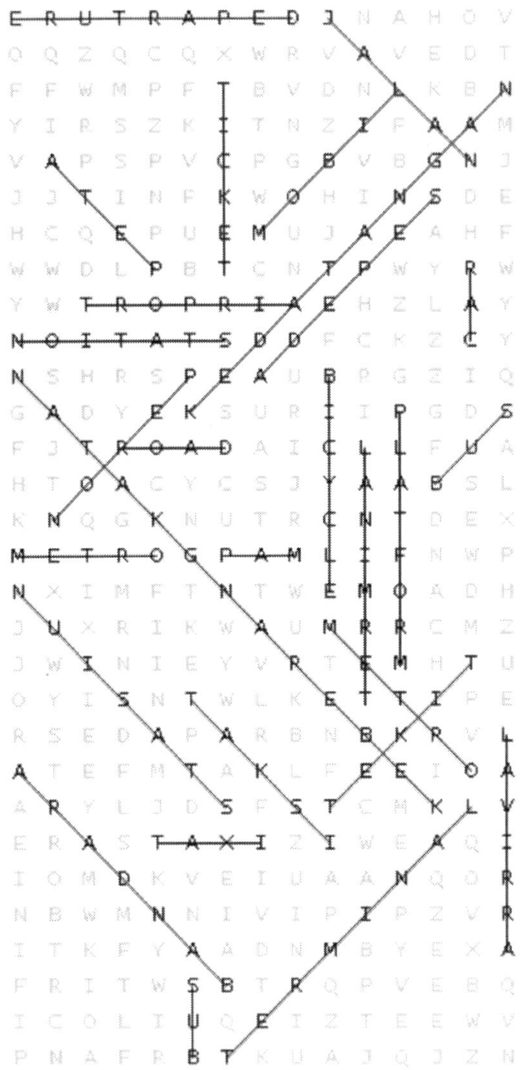

ACCOMMODATIONS

- CHECKING INTO A HOTEL -
- ASKING ABOUT ROOM AMENITIES -
- REPORTING ISSUES OR MAKING REQUESTS -

Hotel Check-In

233. I have a reservation under [Name].
Saya memiliki reservasi atas nama [Nama].
(Sah-yah meh-mee-lee-kee reh-ser-va-see ah-tahs nah-mah [Nah-mah].)

234. Can I see some identification, please?
Boleh saya melihat identitas Anda, tolong?
(Boh-leh sah-yah meh-lee-haht een-den-tee-tahs Ahn-dah, toh-long?)

235. What time is check-in/check-out?
Jam berapa waktu check-in/check-out?
(Jahm beh-rah-pah wahk-too check-in/check-out?)

236. Is breakfast included in the room rate?
Apakah sarapan termasuk dalam tarif kamar?
(Ah-pah-kah sah-rah-pahn tehr-mah-sook dah-lahm tah-reef kah-mahr?)

237. Do you need a credit card for incidentals?
Apakah Anda memerlukan kartu kredit untuk biaya tambahan?
(Ah-pah-kah Ahn-dah meh-mehr-loo-kahn kar-too kre-deet oon-took bee-ah-yah tam-bah-hahn?)

238. May I have a room key, please?
Boleh saya mendapatkan kunci kamar, tolong?
(Boh-leh sah-yah mehn-dah-pah-tahn koon-chee kah-mahr, toh-long?)

239. Is there a shuttle service to the airport?
Apakah ada layanan shuttle ke bandara?
(Ah-pah-kah ah-dah lah-yah-nahn shuttle keh bahn-dah-rah?)

240. Could you call a bellhop for assistance?
Bisakah Anda memanggil petugas bellhop untuk bantuan?
(Bee-sah-kah Ahn-dah meh-mahng-geel peh-too-gahs bellhop oon-took bahn-too-ahn?)

Fun Fact: Lake Toba eruption might have affected global climate.

Room Amenities

241. Can I request a non-smoking room?
Bisakah saya meminta kamar bebas rokok?
(Bee-sah-kah sah-yah meh-meen-tah kah-mahr beh-bahs roh-kohk?)

242. Is there a mini-fridge in the room?
Apakah ada mini kulkas di kamar?
(Ah-pah-kah ah-dah mee-nee kool-kahs dee kah-mahr?)

243. Do you provide free Wi-Fi access?
Apakah Anda menyediakan akses Wi-Fi gratis?
(Ah-pah-kah Ahn-dah meh-nyeh-dee-ah-kahn ahk-ses Wee-Fee grah-tees?)

244. Can I have an extra pillow or blanket?
Bisakah saya mendapatkan bantal atau selimut tambahan?
(Bee-sah-kah sah-yah mehn-dah-pah-tahn bahn-tahl ah-tow seh-lee-moot tam-bah-hahn?)

245. Is there a hairdryer in the bathroom?
Apakah ada pengering rambut di kamar mandi?
(Ah-pah-kah ah-dah pehng-eh-ring rahm-boot dee kah-mahr mahn-dee?)

246. What's the TV channel lineup?
Apa daftar saluran TV?
(Ah-pah dahf-tahr sah-loo-rahn TV?)

247. Are toiletries like shampoo provided?
Apakah perlengkapan mandi seperti sampo disediakan?
(Ah-pah-kah pehr-lehng-kah-pahn mahn-dee seh-pehr-tee sham-poh dee-seh-dee-ah-kahn?)

248. Is room service available 24/7?
Apakah layanan kamar tersedia 24 jam setiap hari?
(Ah-pah-kah lah-yah-nahn kah-mahr tehr-seh-dee-ah 24 jahm seh-tee-ahp hah-ree?)

> **Fun Fact:** The Dragon Blood Tree is found in Indonesia and the tree's resin is used in various products.

Reporting Issues

249. There's a problem with the air conditioning.
Ada masalah dengan AC.
(Ah-dah mah-sah-lah dehng-ahn AC.)

250. The shower is not working properly.
Shower tidak berfungsi dengan baik.
(Show-er tee-dahk behr-foong-see dehng-ahn bighk.)

251. My room key card isn't functioning.
Kartu kunci kamar saya tidak berfungsi.
(Kar-too koon-chee kah-mahr sah-yah tee-dahk behr-foong-see.)

252. There's a leak in the bathroom.
Ada kebocoran di kamar mandi.
(Ah-dah keh-boh-choh-rahn dee kah-mahr mahn-dee.)

253. The TV remote is not responding.
Remote TV tidak merespons.
(Reh-moht TV tee-dahk meh-rehs-pons.)

254. Can you fix the broken light in my room?
Bisakah Anda memperbaiki lampu rusak di kamar saya?
(Bee-sah-kah Ahn-dah mehm-pehr-bah-ee-kee lahmpoo roo-sahk dee kah-mahr sah-yah?)

255. I need assistance with my luggage.
Saya membutuhkan bantuan dengan bagasi saya.
(Sah-yah mehm-boo-tooh-kahn bahn-too-ahn dehng-ahn bah-gah-see sah-yah.)

256. There's a strange noise coming from next door.
Ada suara aneh dari kamar sebelah.
(Ah-dah soo-ah-rah ah-neh dah-ree kah-mahr seh-beh-lah.)

Making Requests

257. Can I have a wake-up call at 7 AM?
Bisakah saya mendapatkan panggilan bangun tidur jam 7 pagi?
(Bee-sah-kah sah-yah mehn-dah-pah-tahn pahng-gee-lahn bahng-oon tee-door jahm too-joo pah-gee?)

> **Fun Fact:** The Mentawai Islands are known for their unique culture and surfing spots.

258. Please send extra towels to my room.
Tolong kirimkan handuk tambahan ke kamarku.
(Toh-long kee-reem-kahn hahn-dook tam-bah-hahn keh kah-mahr-koo.)

259. Could you arrange a taxi for tomorrow?
Bisakah Anda mengatur taksi untuk besok?
(Bee-sah-kah Ahn-dah mehng-ah-toor tak-see oon-took beh-sok?)

260. I'd like to extend my stay for two more nights.
Saya ingin memperpanjang masa inap saya dua malam lagi.
(Sah-yah een-geen mehm-pehr-pahn-jahng mah-sah een-ap sah-yah doo-ah mah-lahm lah-gee.)

> **Idiomatic Expression:** "Kambing hitam." -
> Meaning: "A scapegoat."
> (Literal translation: "Black goat.")

261. Is it possible to change my room?
Apakah mungkin mengganti kamarku?
(Ah-pah-kah moong-keen mehng-gahn-tee kah-mahr-koo?)

262. Can I have a late check-out at 2 PM?
Bisakah saya check-out terlambat pukul 2 siang?
(Bee-sah-kah sah-yah check-out tehr-lahm-baht poo-kool doo see-ahng?)

263. I need an iron and ironing board.
Saya membutuhkan setrika dan papan setrika.
(Sah-yah mehm-boo-tooh-kahn seh-tree-kah dahn pah-pahn seh-tree-kah.)

264. Could you provide directions to [location]?
Bisakah Anda memberikan petunjuk arah ke [lokasi]?
(Bee-sah-kah Ahn-dah mehm-beh-ree-kahn peh-toon-joohk ah-rah keh [loh-kah-see]?)

Room Types and Preferences

265. I'd like to book a single room, please.
Tolong, saya ingin memesan kamar single.
(Toh-long, sah-yah een-geen meh-meh-sahn kah-mahr seeng-gleh.)

266. Do you have any suites available?
Apakah ada suite yang tersedia?
(Ah-pah-kah ah-dah sweet yahng tehr-seh-dee-ah?)

267. Is there a room with a view of the city?
Apakah ada kamar dengan pemandangan kota?
(Ah-pah-kah ah-dah kah-mahr dehng-ahn peh-mahn-dahng-ahn koh-tah?)

268. Is breakfast included in the room rate?
Apakah sarapan termasuk dalam tarif kamar?
(Ah-pah-kah sah-rah-pahn tehr-mah-sook dah-lahm tah-reef kah-mahr?)

269. Can I request a room on a higher floor?
Bisakah saya meminta kamar di lantai yang lebih tinggi?
(Bee-sah-kah sah-yah meh-meen-tah kah-mahr dee lahn-tie yahng leh-beer teen-gee?)

270. Is there an option for a smoking room?
Apakah ada pilihan kamar untuk merokok?
(Ah-pah-kah ah-dah pee-lee-hahn kah-mahr oon-took meh-roh-kok?)

Travel Story: On a crowded bus in Surabaya, a local said, "Rumput tetangga selalu lebih hijau," or "The neighbor's grass is always greener," discussing the allure of foreign lands.

271. Are there connecting rooms for families?
Apakah ada kamar terhubung untuk keluarga?
(Ah-pah-kah ah-dah kah-mahr tehr-hoo-boong oon-took keh-loo-ahr-gah?)

272. I'd prefer a king-size bed.
Saya lebih memilih tempat tidur ukuran king-size.
(Sah-yah leh-beeh meh-mee-leeh tehm-paht tee-dur oo-koo-rahn king-size.)

273. Is there a bathtub in any of the rooms?
Apakah di salah satu kamar ada bathtub?
(Ah-pah-kah dee sah-lah sah-too kah-mahr ah-dah bath-tub?)

Hotel Facilities and Services

274. What time does the hotel restaurant close?
Jam berapa restoran hotel tutup?
(Jahm beh-rah-pah res-toh-rahn ho-tel too-toop?)

275. Is there a fitness center in the hotel?
Apakah di hotel ada pusat kebugaran?
(Ah-pah-kah dee ho-tel ah-dah poo-saht keh-boo-gah-rahn?)

276. Can I access the pool as a guest?
Sebagai tamu, bisakah saya menggunakan kolam renang?
(Seh-bah-guy tah-moo, bee-sah-kah sah-yah mehng-goo-nah-kahn koh-lahm reh-nahng?)

277. Do you offer laundry facilities?
Apakah Anda menyediakan fasilitas laundry?
(Ah-pah-kah Ahn-dah meh-nyeh-dee-ah-kahn fah-see-lee-tahs laun-dry?)

278. Is parking available on-site?
Apakah ada tempat parkir di hotel?
(Ah-pah-kah ah-dah tehm-paht pahr-keer dee ho-tel?)

279. Is room cleaning provided daily?
Apakah pembersihan kamar dilakukan setiap hari?
(Ah-pah-kah pehm-behr-see-hahn kah-mahr dee-lah-koo-kahn seh-tee-ahp hah-ree?)

280. Can I use the business center?
Bisakah saya menggunakan pusat bisnis?
(Bee-sah-kah sah-yah mehng-goo-nah-kahn poo-saht bees-nees?)

281. Are pets allowed in the hotel?
Apakah hotel mengizinkan hewan peliharaan?
(Ah-pah-kah ho-tel mehng-ee-zeen-kahn heh-wahn peh-lee-hah-rahn?)

> **Travel Story:** While exploring the spice markets of Maluku, a vendor explained the diversity of spices as "Seperti bunga yang berbeda tetapi satu jadi," meaning "Like different flowers but united."

Payment and Check-Out

282. Can I have the bill, please?
Bisa saya minta tagihannya, tolong?
(Bee-sah sah-yah meen-tah tah-gee-hahn-nyah, toh-long?)

283. Do you accept credit cards?
Apakah Anda menerima kartu kredit?
(Ah-pah-kah Ahn-dah meh-neh-rah-mah kar-too kreh-deet?)

284. Can I pay in cash?
Bisakah saya membayar dengan tunai?
(Bee-sah-kah sah-yah mehm-bah-yahr dehng-ahn too-nigh?)

285. Is there a security deposit required?
Apakah diperlukan deposit keamanan?
(Ah-pah-kah dee-pehr-loo-kahn deh-poh-seet keh-ah-mah-nahn?)

286. Can I get a receipt for my stay?
Bisakah saya mendapatkan tanda terima untuk menginap saya?
(Bee-sah-kah sah-yah mehn-dah-pah-tahn tahn-dah teh-ree-mah oon-took mehn-gee-nap sah-yah?)

287. What's the check-out time?
Jam berapa waktu check-out?
(Jahm beh-rah-pah wahk-too check-out?)

288. Is late check-out an option?
Apakah check-out terlambat menjadi pilihan?
(Ah-pah-kah check-out tehr-lahm-baht mehn-jah-dee pee-lee-hahn?)

289. Can I settle my bill in advance?
Bisakah saya melunasi tagihan saya terlebih dahulu?
(Bee-sah-kah sah-yah meh-loo-nah-see tah-gee-hahn sah-yah tehr-leh-beeh dah-hoo-loo?)

Booking Accommodations

290. I'd like to make a reservation.
Saya ingin membuat reservasi.
(Sah-yah een-geen mehm-boo-aht reh-ser-va-see.)

291. How much is the room rate per night?
Berapa tarif kamar per malam?
(Beh-rah-pah tah-reef kah-mahr pehr mah-lahm?)

292. Can I book online or by phone?
Bisakah saya memesan secara online atau melalui telepon?
(Bee-sah-kah sah-yah meh-meh-sahn sehk-ah-rah on-line ah-tow meh-lah-loo-ee teh-leh-pon?)

293. Are there any special promotions?
Apakah ada promosi khusus?
(Ah-pah-kah ah-dah proh-moh-see koo-soos?)

294. Is breakfast included in the booking?
Apakah sarapan termasuk dalam pemesanan?
(Ah-pah-kah sah-rah-pahn tehr-mah-sook dah-lahm peh-meh-sah-nahn?)

295. Can you confirm my reservation?
Bisakah Anda mengonfirmasi reservasi saya?
(Bee-sah-kah Ahn-dah mehng-ohn-feer-mah-see reh-ser-va-see sah-yah?)

296. What's the cancellation policy?
Apa kebijakan pembatalan?
(Ah-pah keh-bee-jah-kahn pehm-bah-tah-lahn?)

297. I'd like to modify my booking.
Saya ingin mengubah pemesanan saya.
(Sah-yah een-geen mehng-oo-bah peh-meh-sah-nahn sah-yah.)

"Kecil-kecil cabe rawit."
"Small but spicy like a bird's eye chili."
Describing someone small but feisty or capable.

Mini Lesson:
Basic Grammar Principles in Indonesian #1

Introduction:

Indonesian, a language spoken by millions in Indonesia and recognized for its simplicity in terms of grammatical structure, is an Austronesian language. It is known for not having complex verb conjugations or noun declensions, making it accessible for learners. This lesson provides an introduction to the fundamental grammar concepts of Indonesian, essential for beginners starting their journey into learning this fascinating language.

1. Nouns:

Indonesian nouns do not have genders, plural forms, or articles. Plurality is often indicated by context or the use of quantifiers:

- *Anjing (a dog/dogs)*
- *Rumah (a house/houses)*

2. Personal Pronouns:

Indonesian has a range of personal pronouns often based on the formality of the context:

- *Saya (I/me - formal)*
- *Aku (I/me - informal)*
- *Anda (you - formal)*

- *Kamu (you - informal)*
- *Dia (he/she)*
- *Kami (we/us - excluding the listener)*
- *Kita (we/us - including the listener)*
- *Mereka (they/them)*

3. Verb Usage:

Verbs in Indonesian do not conjugate according to subject or tense. Time is often indicated by time-specific words or context:

- *Saya makan (I eat/I am eating)*
- *Saya akan makan (I will eat)*
- *Saya sudah makan (I have eaten)*

4. Tenses:

Tense in Indonesian is understood through context and time indicators rather than verb changes:

- *Sekarang (now)*
- *Kemarin (yesterday)*
- *Besok (tomorrow)*

5. Negation:

Negation is typically done using "tidak" (not) before the verb:

- *Saya tidak mengerti (I don't understand)*
- *Dia tidak berbicara Bahasa Indonesia (He/She does not speak Indonesian)*

6. Questions:

Questions can be formed by adding question words at the beginning or end of a sentence:

- *Apa (what)*
- *Dimana (where)*
- *Kapan (when)*
- *Bagaimana (how)*
- *Apakah Anda berbicara Bahasa Indonesia? (Do you speak Indonesian?)*
- *Di mana kamar mandi? (Where is the bathroom?)*

7. Plurals:

Plurals are often indicated by repeating the noun or using words like "beberapa" (some) or "banyak" (many):

- *Buku-buku (books)*
- *Beberapa orang (some people)*

Conclusion:

Understanding these fundamental aspects of Indonesian grammar will significantly aid in learning the language. Consistency in practice, along with engagement in Indonesian-speaking environments, will enhance your skills. Selamat belajar! (Happy learning!)

SHOPPING

- BARGAINING AND HAGGLING -
- DESCRIBING ITEMS AND SIZES -
- MAKING PURCHASES AND PAYMENTS -

Bargaining

298. Can you give me a discount?
Bisakah Anda memberikan saya diskon?
(Bee-sah-kah Ahn-dah mehm-beh-ree-kahn sah-yah dees-kohn?)

299. What's your best price?
Berapa harga terbaik Anda?
(Beh-rah-pah hahr-gah tehr-bah-ik Ahn-dah?)

300. Is this the final price?
Apakah ini harga akhir?
(Ah-pah-kah ee-nee hahr-gah ah-keer?)

301. What's the lowest you can go?
Berapa harga terendah yang bisa Anda tawarkan?
(Beh-rah-pah hahr-gah teh-rehn-dah yahng bee-sah Ahn-dah tah-war-kahn?)

302. Can you do any better on the price?
Bisakah Anda memberikan harga yang lebih baik?
(Bee-sah-kah Ahn-dah mehm-beh-ree-kahn hahr-gah yahng leh-beeh bah-ik?)

303. Are there any promotions or deals?
Apakah ada promosi atau kesepakatan?
(Ah-pah-kah ah-dah proh-moh-see ah-tow keh-seh-pah-kah-tahn?)

304. I'm on a budget. Can you lower the price?
Saya memiliki anggaran terbatas. Bisakah Anda menurunkan harga?
(Sah-yah meh-mee-lee-kee ahng-gah-rahn tehr-bah-tahs. Bee-sah-kah Ahn-dah meh-noo-roon-kahn hahr-gah?)

305. I'd like to negotiate the price.
Saya ingin menawar harga.
(Sah-yah een-geen meh-nah-war hahr-gah.)

306. Do you offer any discounts for cash payments?
Apakah Anda memberikan diskon untuk pembayaran tunai?
(Ah-pah-kah Ahn-dah mehm-beh-ree-kahn dees-kohn oon-took pehm-bah-yah-rahn too-nigh?)

307. Can you match the price from your competitor?
Bisakah Anda menyesuaikan harga dengan pesaing Anda?
(Bee-sah-kah Ahn-dah mehn-ye-soo-ah-ee-kahn hahr-gah dehng-ahn peh-sah-eeng Ahn-dah?)

Item Descriptions

308. Can you tell me about this product?
Bisakah Anda memberikan informasi tentang produk ini?
(Bee-sah-kah Ahn-dah mehm-beh-ree-kahn een-for-mah-see tehn-tahng proh-duk ee-nee?)

309. What are the specifications of this item?
Apa spesifikasi dari produk ini?
(Ah-pah speh-see-fee-kah-see dah-ree proh-duk ee-nee?)

310. Is this available in different colors?
Apakah produk ini tersedia dalam berbagai warna?
(Ah-pah-kah proh-duk ee-nee tehr-seh-dee-ah dah-lahm behr-bah-guy war-nah?)

311. Can you explain how this works?
Bisakah Anda menjelaskan cara kerjanya?
(Bee-sah-kah Ahn-dah mehn-jeh-lahs-kahn chah-rah kehr-jah-nyah?)

312. What's the material of this item?
Apa bahan dari produk ini?
(Ah-pah bah-hahn dah-ree proh-duk ee-nee?)

313. Are there any warranties or guarantees?
Apakah produk ini memiliki garansi atau jaminan?
(Ah-pah-kah proh-duk ee-nee meh-mee-lee gah-ran-see ah-tow jah-mee-nahn?)

314. Does it come with accessories?
Apakah produk ini disertai dengan aksesori?
(Ah-pah-kah proh-duk ee-nee dee-sehr-tie dehng-ahn ahk-seh-soh-ree?)

315. Can you show me how to use this?
Bisakah Anda menunjukkan cara menggunakannya?
(Bee-sah-kah Ahn-dah meh-noon-jook-kahn chah-rah mehng-goo-nah-kahn-nyah?)

316. Are there any size options available?
Apakah tersedia pilihan ukuran?
(Ah-pah-kah tehr-seh-dee-ah pee-lee-hahn oo-koo-rahn?)

317. Can you describe the features of this product?
Bisakah Anda menjelaskan fitur-fitur produk ini?
(Bee-sah-kah Ahn-dah mehn-jeh-lahs-kahn fee-toor-fee-toor proh-duk ee-nee?)

Payments

318. I'd like to pay with a credit card.
Saya ingin membayar dengan kartu kredit.
(Sah-yah een-geen mehm-bah-yahr dehng-ahn kar-too kreh-deet.)

319. Do you accept debit cards?
Apakah Anda menerima kartu debit?
(Ah-pah-kah Ahn-dah meh-meh-rah-nah kar-too deh-beet?)

320. Can I pay in cash?
Bisakah saya membayar dengan tunai?
(Bee-sah-kah sah-yah mehm-bah-yahr dehng-ahn too-nigh?)

> **Idiomatic Expression:** "Menggarami laut." - Meaning: "Doing something pointless." (Literal translation: "Salting the sea.")

321. What's your preferred payment method?
Apa metode pembayaran yang Anda sukai?
(Ah-pah meh-toh-deh pehm-bah-yoo-rah-ahn yahng Ahn-dah soo-kigh?)

322. Is there an extra charge for using a card?
Apakah ada biaya tambahan untuk menggunakan kartu?
(Ah-pah-kah ah-dah bee-ah-yah tam-bah-hahn oon-took mehng-goo-nah-kahn kar-too?)

323. Can I split the payment into installments?
Bisakah saya membagi pembayaran menjadi cicilan?
(Bee-sah-kah sah-yah mehm-bah-gee pehm-bah-yoo-rah-ahn mehn-jah-dee chee-chee-lahn?)

324. Do you offer online payment options?
Apakah Anda menyediakan opsi pembayaran online?
(Ah-pah-kah Ahn-dah meh-nyeh-dee-ah-kahn op-see pehm-bah-yoo-rah-ahn on-line?)

325. Can I get a receipt for this purchase?
Bisakah saya mendapatkan struk untuk pembelian ini?
(Bee-sah-kah sah-yah mehn-dah-pah-tahn strook oon-took pehm-bee-lee-ahn ee-nee?)

326. Are there any additional fees?
Apakah ada biaya tambahan?
(Ah-pah-kah ah-dah bee-ah-yah tam-bah-hahn?)

327. Is there a minimum purchase amount for card payments?
Apakah ada jumlah pembelian minimum untuk pembayaran kartu?
(Ah-pah-kah ah-dah joo-mah-lah pehm-beh-lee-ahn mee-nee-moom oon-took pehm-bah-yah-rahn kahr-too?)

> **Travel Story:** In a traditional dance performance in Bali, the dancer described her art as "Air tenang menghanyutkan," meaning "Still waters run deep," to express the depth of her cultural heritage.

Asking for Recommendations

328. Can you recommend something popular?
Bisakah Anda merekomendasikan sesuatu yang populer?
(Bee-sah-kah Ahn-dah meh-reh-koh-men-dah-sah-kahn seh-soo-ah-too yahng poh-poo-ler?)

329. What's your best-selling product?
Apa produk terlaris Anda?
(Ah-pah proh-duk tehr-lah-rees Ahn-dah?)

330. Do you have any customer favorites?
Apakah Anda memiliki favorit pelanggan?
(Ah-pah-kah Ahn-dah meh-mee-lee fah-vo-reet peh-lahng-gahn?)

331. Is there a brand you would suggest?
Apakah ada merek yang Anda sarankan?
(Ah-pah-kah ah-dah meh-rek yahng Ahn-dah sahr-ahn-kahn?)

332. Could you point me to high-quality items?
Bisakah Anda menunjukkan saya barang berkualitas tinggi?
(Bee-sah-kah Ahn-dah meh-noon-jook-kahn sah-yah bahr-ahng behr-koo-ah-lee-tahs teen-gee?)

333. What do most people choose in this category?
Apa yang kebanyakan orang pilih dalam kategori ini?
(Ah-pah yahng keh-bahn-yah-kahn oh-rahng pee-leeh dah-lahm kah-teh-go-ree ee-nee?)

334. Are there any special recommendations?
Apakah ada rekomendasi khusus?
(Ah-pah-kah ah-dah reh-koh-men-dah-see koo-soos?)

335. Can you tell me what's trendy right now?
Bisakah Anda memberitahu saya apa yang sedang tren saat ini?
(Bee-sah-kah Ahn-dah mehm-beh-ree-tah-hoo sah-yah ah-pah yahng seh-dahng tren sah-at ee-nee?)

336. What's your personal favorite here?
Apa favorit pribadi Anda di sini?
(Ah-pah fah-vo-reet pree-bah-dee Ahn-dah dee see-nee?)

337. Any suggestions for a gift?
Ada saran untuk hadiah?
(Ah-dah sah-rahn oon-took hah-dee-ah?)

Language Learning Tip: Translate Songs - Translate Indonesian songs to understand the meaning.

Returns and Exchanges

338. I'd like to return this item.
Saya ingin mengembalikan produk ini.
(Sah-yah een-geen meng-em-bah-lee-kahn proh-duk ee-nee.)

339. Can I exchange this for a different size?
Bisakah saya menukar ini dengan ukuran lain?
(Bee-sah-kah sah-yah meh-noo-kahr ee-nee dehng-ahn oo-koo-rahn lie-in?)

340. What's your return policy?
Apa kebijakan pengembalian Anda?
(Ah-pah keh-bee-jah-kahn peng-em-bah-lee-ahn Ahn-dah?)

341. Is there a time limit for returns?
Apakah ada batas waktu untuk pengembalian?
(Ah-pah-kah ah-dah bah-tahs wahk-too oon-took peng-em-bah-lee-ahn?)

342. Do I need a receipt for a return?
Apakah saya memerlukan struk untuk pengembalian?
(Ah-pah-kah sah-yah meh-mehr-loo-kahn strook oon-took peng-em-bah-lee-ahn?)

343. Is there a restocking fee for returns?
Apakah ada biaya restocking untuk pengembalian?
(Ah-pah-kah ah-dah bee-ah-yah reh-stock-ing oon-took peng-em-bah-lee-ahn?)

344. Can I get a refund or store credit?
Bisakah saya mendapatkan pengembalian uang atau kredit toko?
(Bee-sah-kah sah-yah mehn-dah-pah-tahn peng-em-bah-lee-ahn oo-ahng ah-tow kreh-deet toh-koh?)

345. Do you offer exchanges without receipts?
Apakah Anda menawarkan penukaran tanpa struk?
(Ah-pah-kah Ahn-dah meh-nah-war-kahn peh-noo-kahr-ahn tahn-pah strook?)

346. What's the process for returning a defective item?
Bagaimana proses pengembalian barang cacat?
(Bah-gigh-mah-nah proh-ses peng-em-bah-lee-ahn bahr-ahng chah-chat?)

347. Can I return an online purchase in-store?
Bisakah saya mengembalikan pembelian online di toko?
(Bee-sah-kah sah-yah meng-em-bah-lee-kahn pem-bee-lee-ahn on-line dee toh-koh?)

> **Travel Story:** On a boat journey in the Thousand Islands, a guide described the archipelago as "Bagai mutiara yang tersebar," meaning "Like scattered pearls," for its beauty and splendor.

Shopping for Souvenirs

348. I'm looking for local souvenirs.
Saya sedang mencari oleh-oleh lokal.
(Sah-yah seh-dahng men-char-ee oh-leh-oh-leh loh-kahl.)

349. What's a popular souvenir from this place?
Apa oleh-oleh populer dari tempat ini?
(Ah-pah oh-leh-oh-leh po-poo-ler dah-ree tem-paht ee-nee?)

350. Do you have any handmade souvenirs?
Apakah Anda memiliki oleh-oleh buatan tangan?
(Ah-pah-kah Ahn-dah meh-mee-lee oh-leh-oh-leh boo-ah-tahn tahn-gahn?)

351. Are there any traditional items here?
Apakah ada barang tradisional di sini?
(Ah-pah-kah ah-dah bahr-ahng trah-dee-see-oh-nahl dee see-nee?)

352. Can you suggest a unique souvenir?
Bisakah Anda merekomendasikan suvenir unik?
(Bee-sah-kah Ahn-dah meh-reh-koh-men-dah-sah-kahn soo-veh-neer oo-neek?)

353. I want something that represents this city.
Saya ingin sesuatu yang mewakili kota ini.
(Sah-yah een-geen seh-soo-ah-too yahng meh-wah-kee-lee koh-tah ee-nee.)

354. Are there souvenirs for a specific landmark?
Apakah ada suvenir untuk landmark tertentu?
(Ah-pah-kah ah-dah soo-veh-neer oon-took lahn-mark tehr-ten-too?)

355. Can you show me souvenirs with cultural significance?
Bisakah Anda menunjukkan suvenir dengan makna budaya?
(Bee-sah-kah Ahn-dah meh-noon-jook-kahn soo-veh-neer dehng-ahn makh-nah boo-dah-yah?)

356. Do you offer personalized souvenirs?
Apakah Anda menawarkan suvenir yang dipersonalisasi?
(Ah-pah-kah Ahn-dah meh-nah-war-kahn soo-veh-neer yahng dee-pehr-soh-nah-lee-sah-see?)

357. What's the price range for souvenirs?
Berapa kisaran harga suvenir?
(Beh-rah-pah kee-sah-rahn hahr-gah soo-veh-neer?)

Cultural Insight: The Javanese royal palaces, known as Kraton, are centers of culture and traditional arts.

Shopping Online

358. How do I place an order online?
Bagaimana cara memesan secara online?
(Bah-gigh-mah-nah chah-rah meh-meh-sahn sehk-ah-rah on-line?)

359. What's the website for online shopping?
Apa situs web untuk belanja online?
(Ah-pah see-toos wehb oon-took beh-lahn-jah on-line?)

360. Do you offer free shipping?
Apakah Anda menawarkan pengiriman gratis?
(Ah-pah-kah Ahn-dah meh-nah-war-kahn peng-kee-ree-mahn grah-tees?)

361. Are there any online discounts or promotions?
Apakah ada diskon atau promosi online?
(Ah-pah-kah ah-dah dees-kohn ah-tow proh-moh-see on-line?)

362. Can I track my online order?
Bisakah saya melacak pesanan online saya?
(Bee-sah-kah sah-yah meh-lah-chahk peh-sah-nahn on-line sah-yah?)

363. What's the return policy for online purchases?
Apa kebijakan pengembalian untuk pembelian online?
(Ah-pah keh-bee-jah-kahn peng-em-bah-lee-ahn oon-took pem-bee-lee-ahn on-line?)

364. Do you accept various payment methods online?
Apakah Anda menerima berbagai metode pembayaran secara online?
(Ah-pah-kah Ahn-dah meh-meh-rah-nah behr-bah-gigh meh-toh-deh pem-bah-yoo-rah-ahn sehk-ah-rah on-line?)

365. Is there a customer support hotline for online orders?
Apakah ada hotline dukungan pelanggan untuk pesanan online?
(*Ah-pah-kah ah-dah hot-line doo-koon-gahn peh-lang-gahn oon-took peh-sah-nahn on-line?)*

Idiomatic Expression: "Menjilat ludah sendiri." - Meaning: "To take back one's words." (Literal translation: "Licking one's own saliva.")

366. Can I change or cancel my online order?
Bisakah saya mengubah atau membatalkan pesanan online saya?
(Bee-sah-kah sah-yah meng-oo-bah ah-tow mehm-bah-tahl-kahn peh-sah-nahn on-line sah-yah?)

367. What's the delivery time for online purchases?
Berapa waktu pengiriman untuk pembelian online?
(Beh-rah-pah wahk-too peng-kee-ree-mahn oon-took pem-bee-lee-ahn on-line?)

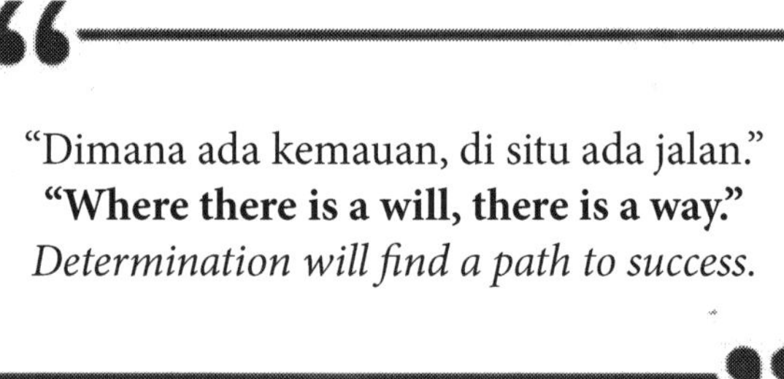

Cross Word Puzzle: Shopping

(Provide the English translation for the following Indonesian words)

Down

2. - HARGA
3. - PENJUALAN
5. - DISKON
7. - KERANJANG
8. - STRUK
9. - PAKAIAN
11. - DOMPET

Across

1. - BELANJA
4. - MEREK
6. - RITEL
7. - PELANGGAN
9. - MEJA
10. - BUTIK
12. - KASIR

Correct Answers:

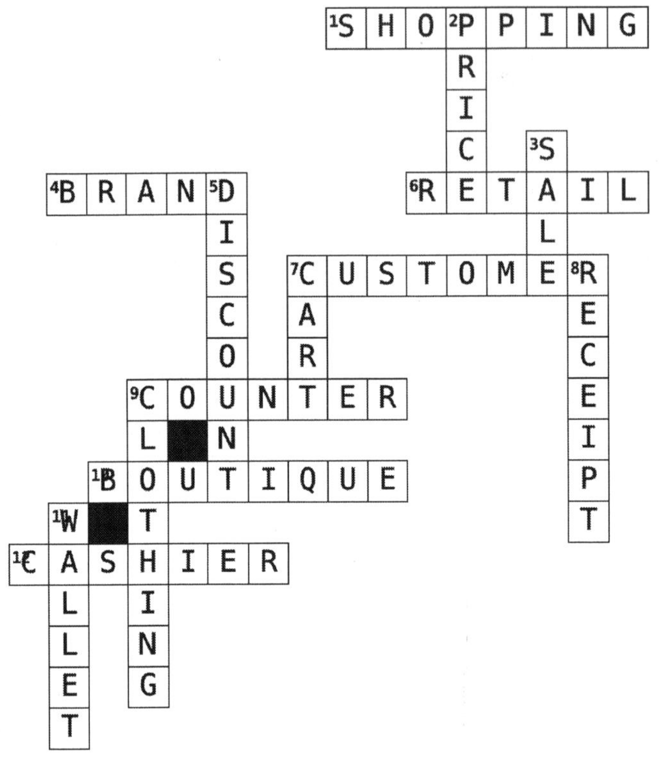

EMERGENCIES

- SEEKING HELP IN CASE OF AN EMERGENCY -
- REPORTING ACCIDENTS OR HEALTH ISSUES -
- CONTACTING AUTHORITIES OR MEDICAL SERVICES -

Getting Help in Emergencies

368. Call an ambulance, please.
Tolong panggilkan ambulans.
(Toh-long pang-geel-kahn ahm-boo-lahns.)

Language Learning Tip: Label Things in Your House - Use sticky notes to label objects in Indonesian.

369. I need a doctor right away.
Saya butuh dokter segera.
(Sah-yah boo-tooh dok-tehr seh-ge-rah.)

370. Is there a hospital nearby?
Apakah ada rumah sakit di dekat sini?
(Ah-pah-kah ah-dah roo-mah sah-keet dee deh-kat see-nee?)

371. Help! I've lost my way.
Tolong! Saya tersesat.
(Toh-long! Sah-yah tehr-seh-saht.)

372. Can you call the police?
Bisakah Anda memanggil polisi?
(Bee-sah-kah Ahn-dah meh-mang-geel poh-lee-see?)

373. Someone, please call for help.
Tolong, seseorang panggilkan bantuan.
(Toh-long, seh-seh-oh-rahng pang-geel-kahn bahn-too-ahn.)

374. My friend is hurt, we need assistance.
Teman saya terluka, kami butuh bantuan.
(Teh-mahn sah-yah tehr-loo-kah, kah-mee boo-tooh bahn-too-ahn.)

375. I've been robbed; I need the authorities.
Saya telah dirampok; saya butuh pihak berwenang.
(Sah-yah teh-lah dee-rahm-pok; sah-yah boo-tooh pee-hahk beer-weh-nahng.)

376. Please, I need immediate assistance.
Tolong, saya butuh bantuan segera.
(Toh-long, sah-yah boo-tooh bahn-too-ahn seh-ge-rah.)

377. Is there a fire station nearby?
Apakah ada stasiun pemadam kebakaran di dekat sini?
(Ah-pah-kah ah-dah stah-see-oon peh-mah-dahm keh-bah-kah-rahn dee deh-kat see-nee?)

Reporting Incidents

378. I've witnessed an accident.
Saya menyaksikan sebuah kecelakaan.
(Sah-yah mehn-yahk-see-kahn seh-boo-ah keh-cheh-lah-kahn.)

379. There's been a car crash.
Telah terjadi kecelakaan mobil.
(Teh-lah tehr-jah-dee keh-cheh-lah-kahn moh-beel.)

380. We need to report a fire.
Kami perlu melaporkan kebakaran.
(Kah-mee pehr-loo meh-lah-pohr-kahn keh-bah-kah-rahn.)

381. Someone has stolen my wallet.
Seseorang telah mencuri dompet saya.
(Seh-seh-oh-rahng teh-lah mehn-choo-ree dohm-peht sah-yah.)

382. I need to report a lost passport.
Saya perlu melaporkan paspor yang hilang.
(Sah-yah pehr-loo meh-lah-pohr-kahn pahs-pohr yahng hee-lahng.)

383. There's a suspicious person here.
Ada orang mencurigakan di sini.
(Ah-dah oh-rahng men-choo-ree-gah-kahn dee see-nee.)

384. I've found a lost child.
Saya menemukan anak yang hilang.
(Sah-yah meh-neh-moo-kahn ah-nahk yahng hee-lahng.)

385. Can you help me report a missing person?
Bisakah Anda membantu saya melaporkan orang yang hilang?
(Bee-sah-kah Ahn-dah mehm-bahn-too sah-yah meh-lah-pohr-kahn oh-rahng yahng hee-lahng?)

386. We've had a break-in at our home.
Rumah kami telah dibobol.
(Roo-mah kah-mee teh-lah dee-boh-bol.)

387. I need to report a damaged vehicle.
Saya perlu melaporkan kendaraan yang rusak.
(Sah-yah pehr-loo meh-lah-pohr-kahn ken-dah-rahn yahng roo-sahk.)

Contacting Authorities

388. I'd like to speak to the police.
Saya ingin berbicara dengan polisi.
(Sah-yah een-geen berr-bee-char-rah dehng-ahn poh-lee-see.)

389. I need to contact the embassy.
Saya perlu menghubungi kedutaan.
(Sah-yah pehr-loo meng-hoo-boong-ee keh-doo-tahn.)

390. Can you connect me to the fire department?
Bisakah Anda menghubungkan saya ke departemen pemadam kebakaran?
(Bee-sah-kah Ahn-dah meng-hoo-boong-kahn sah-yah keh deh-par-teh-men peh-mah-dahm keh-bah-kah-rahn?)

391. We need to reach animal control.
Kami perlu menghubungi kontrol hewan.
(Kah-mee pehr-loo meng-hoo-boong-ee kohn-trohl heh-wahn.)

392. How do I get in touch with the coast guard?
Bagaimana saya bisa menghubungi penjaga pantai?
(Bah-gigh-mah-nah sah-yah bee-sah meng-hoo-boong-ee pehn-jah-gah pahn-tie?)

393. I'd like to report a noise complaint.
Saya ingin melaporkan keluhan tentang kebisingan.
(Sah-yah een-geen meh-lah-pohr-kahn keh-loo-hahn ten-tahng keh-bee-seeng-ahn.)

394. I need to contact child protective services.
Saya perlu menghubungi layanan perlindungan anak.
(Sah-yah pehr-loo meng-hoo-boong-ee lay-ah-nahn pehr-leen-doong-ahn ah-nahk.)

395. Is there a hotline for disaster relief?
Apakah ada hotline untuk bantuan bencana?
(Ah-pah-kah ah-dah hot-line oon-took bahn-too-ahn ben-chah-nah?)

Fun Fact: Indonesia is home to rare animals like the Javan rhinoceros.

396. I want to report a hazardous situation.
Saya ingin melaporkan situasi berbahaya.
(Sah-yah een-geen meh-lah-pohr-kahn see-too-ah-see berr-bah-hah-yah.)

397. I need to reach the environmental agency.
Saya perlu menghubungi badan lingkungan.
(Sah-yah pehr-loo meng-hoo-boong-ee bah-dahn leeng-koon-gahn.)

> **Travel Story:** During a rainforest trek in Kalimantan, a guide referred to the dense jungle as "Bagaikan hutan belantara," literally "Like a dense forest," symbolizing life's complexities.

Medical Emergencies

398. I'm feeling very ill.
Saya merasa sangat sakit.
(Sah-yah meh-rah-sah sahng-ahht sah-keet.)

399. There's been an accident; we need a medic.
Telah terjadi kecelakaan; kami membutuhkan bantuan medis.
(Teh-lah tehr-jah-dee keh-cheh-lah-kahn; kah-mee mem-boo-tooh-kahn bahn-too-ahn meh-dees.)

400. Call 112; it's a medical emergency.
Hubungi 112; ini adalah keadaan darurat medis.
(Hoo-boong-ee sah-tooh-blahs; ee-nee ah-dah-lah keh-ah-dahn dah-oo-rahht meh-dees.)

> **Fun Fact:** Lake Toba is the largest volcanic lake globally, formed by a massive supervolcanic eruption.

401. We need an ambulance right away.
Kami butuh ambulans segera.
(Kah-mee boo-tooh ahm-boo-lahns seh-ge-rah.)

402. I'm having trouble breathing.
Saya kesulitan bernapas.
(Sah-yah keh-soo-lee-tahn berr-nah-pahs.)

403. Someone has lost consciousness.
Seseorang telah pingsan.
(Seh-seh-oh-rahng teh-lah peeng-sahn.)

404. I think it's a heart attack; call for help.
Saya pikir ini serangan jantung; panggil bantuan.
(Sah-yah pee-keer ee-nee seh-rahng-gahn jahn-toong; pahng-geel bahn-too-ahn.)

405. There's been a severe injury.
Telah terjadi cedera parah.
(Teh-lah tehr-jah-dee cheh-deh-rah pah-rah.)

406. I need immediate medical attention.
Saya memerlukan perawatan medis segera.
(Sah-yah meh-mehr-loo-kahn peh-rah-wah-tahn meh-dees seh-ge-rah.)

407. Is there a first-aid station nearby?
Apakah ada pos P3K di dekat sini?
(Ah-pah-kah ah-dah pohs peh-ti-gah-kah dee deh-kat see-nee?)

> **Idiomatic Expression:** "Kayu sudah menjadi abu." - Meaning: "What's done is done."
> (Literal translation: "Wood has become ash.")

Fire and Safety

408. There's a fire; call 112!
Ada kebakaran; hubungi 112!
(Ah-dah keh-bah-kah-rahn; hoo-boong-gee sah-tooh-blahs!)

409. We need to evacuate the building.
Kita perlu mengosongkan gedung.
(Kee-tah pehr-loo meng-goh-song-kahn ge-doong.)

410. Fire extinguisher, quick!
Alat pemadam api, cepat!
(Ah-laht peh-mah-dahm ah-pee, cheh-paht!)

411. I smell gas; we need to leave.
Saya mencium gas; kita harus keluar.
(Sah-yah men-choo-eem gahs; kee-tah hah-roos keh-loo-ahr.)

Fun Fact: The Rafflesia arnoldii, found in Indonesia, is the world's largest flower.

412. Can you contact the fire department?
Bisa menghubungi pemadam kebakaran?
(Bee-sah meng-hoo-boong-gee peh-mah-dahm keh-bah-kah-rahn?)

413. There's a hazardous spill; we need help.
Ada tumpahan berbahaya; kita membutuhkan bantuan.
(Ah-dah toom-pah-hahn berr-bah-hah-yah; kee-tah mem-boo-tooh-kahn bahn-too-ahn.)

414. Is there a fire escape route?
Apakah ada jalur evakuasi kebakaran?
(Ah-pah-kah ah-dah jah-loor eh-vah-koo-ah-see keh-bah-kah-rahn?)

415. This area is not safe; we need to move.
Area ini tidak aman; kita perlu bergerak.
(Ah-ray-ah ee-nee tee-dahk ah-mahn; kee-tah pehr-loo berr-geh-rahk.)

416. Alert, there's a potential explosion.
Waspada, ada potensi ledakan.
(Wahs-pah-dah, ah-dah poh-ten-see leh-dah-kahn.)

417. I see smoke; we need assistance.
Saya melihat asap; kita membutuhkan bantuan.
(Sah-yah meh-lee-haht ah-sahp; kee-tah mem-boo-tooh-kahn bahn-too-ahn.)

Natural Disasters

418. It's an earthquake; take cover!
Ini gempa bumi; cari perlindungan!
(Ee-nee gemp-ah boo-mee; chah-ree pehr-leen-doong-gahn!)

419. We're experiencing a tornado; find shelter.
Ada tornado; cari tempat berlindung.
(Ah-dah tor-nah-doh; chah-ree tem-paht berr-leen-doong.)

420. Flood warning; move to higher ground.
Peringatan banjir; pindah ke tempat yang lebih tinggi.
(Peh-reen-gah-tahn bahn-jeer; peen-dah keh tem-paht yahng leh-beeh teeng-gee.)

421. We need to prepare for a hurricane.
Kita perlu bersiap untuk badai.
(Kee-tah pehr-loo berr-see-ahp oon-took bah-die.)

422. This is a tsunami alert; head inland.
Ini adalah peringatan tsunami; menuju ke daratan.
(Ee-nee ah-dah-lah peh-reen-gah-tahn tsoo-nah-mee; meh-noo-joo keh dah-rah-tahn.)

Fun Fact: Indonesia is home to approximately 130 active volcanoes.

423. It's a wildfire; evacuate immediately.
Ini kebakaran hutan; segera evakuasi.
(Ee-nee keh-bah-kah-rahn hoo-tahn; seh-geh-rah eh-vah-koo-ah-see.)

424. There's a volcanic eruption; take precautions.
Ada letusan gunung berapi; ambil tindakan pencegahan.
(Ah-dah leh-too-sahn goon-oong beh-rah-pee; ahm-beel teen-dah-kahn pehn-cheh-gah-hahn.)

425. We've had an avalanche; help needed.
Terjadi longsoran salju; butuh bantuan.
(Tehr-jah-dee lohng-soh-rahn sahl-joo; boo-tooh bahn-too-ahn.)

426. Earthquake aftershock; stay indoors.
Gempa susulan; tetap di dalam.
(Gehm-pah soo-soo-lahn; teh-tahp dee dah-lahm.)

427. Severe thunderstorm; seek shelter.
Badai petir hebat; cari tempat perlindungan.
(Bah-die peh-teer heh-baht; chah-ree tem-paht pehr-leen-doong-gahn.)

Idiomatic Expression: "Mulut manis." -
Meaning: "Flattering."
(Literal translation: "Sweet mouth.")

Emergency Services Information

428. What's the emergency hotline number?
Berapa nomor hotline darurat?
(Beh-rah-pah noh-mor hoht-leen dah-roo-raht?)

429. Where's the nearest police station?
Di mana kantor polisi terdekat?
(Dee mah-nah kahn-tohr poh-lee-see tehr-deh-kaht?)

430. How do I contact the fire department?
Bagaimana cara menghubungi pemadam kebakaran?
(Bah-gai-mah-nah chah-rah meng-hoo-boong-ee peh-mah-dahm keh-bah-kah-rahn?)

431. Is there a hospital nearby?
Apakah ada rumah sakit terdekat?
(Ah-pah-kah ah-dah roo-mah sah-keet tehr-deh-kaht?)

432. What's the number for poison control?
Berapa nomor pusat kontrol racun?
(Beh-rah-pah noh-mor poo-saht kohn-trol rah-choon?)

433. Where can I find a disaster relief center?
Di mana saya bisa menemukan pusat bantuan bencana?
(Dee mah-nah sah-yah bee-sah meh-neh-moo-kahn poo-saht bahn-too-ahn behn-chah-nah?)

Fun Fact: Indonesia has around 40,000 species of flowering plants.

434. What's the local emergency radio station?
Stasiun radio darurat lokal apa?
(*Stah-see-oon rah-dee-oh dah-roo-raht loh-kahl ah-pah?)*

435. Are there any shelters in the area?
Apakah ada tempat perlindungan di area ini?
(Ah-pah-kah ah-dah tem-paht pehr-leen-doong-gahn dee ah-ree-ah ee-nee?)

436. Who do I call for road assistance?
Siapa yang harus saya hubungi untuk bantuan di jalan?
(See-ah-pah yahng hah-roos sah-yah hoo-boong-gee oon-took bahn-too-ahn dee jah-lahn?)

437. How can I reach search and rescue teams?
Bagaimana cara menghubungi tim pencarian dan penyelamatan?
(*Bah-gai-mah-nah chah-rah meng-hoo-boong-gee teem pen-chah-ree-ahn dahn pehn-yeh-lah-mah-tahn?)*

> "Biar lambat asal selamat."
> **"Better to be slow as long as it's safe."**
> *It's better to be cautious and safe than to rush and make mistakes.*

Interactive Challenge: Emergencies Quiz

1. **How do you say "emergency" in Indonesian?**

    a) Apel
    b) Keadaan Darurat
    c) Keju
    d) Pantai

2. **What's the Indonesian word for "ambulance"?**

    a) Mobil
    b) Sepeda
    c) Ambulans
    d) Sekolah

3. **If you need immediate medical attention, what should you say in Indonesian?**

    a) Saya ingin roti.
    b) Di mana stasiunnya?
    c) Saya membutuhkan bantuan medis segera.

4. **How do you ask "Is there a hospital nearby?" in Indonesian?**

    a) Di mana bioskop?
    b) Apakah Anda memiliki pena?
    c) Apakah ada rumah sakit di dekat sini?

5. **What's the Indonesian word for "police"?**

    a) Apel
    b) Polisi
    c) Kereta

6. **How do you say "fire" in Indonesian?**

   a) Matahari
   b) Anjing
   c) Api
   d) Buku

7. **If you've witnessed an accident, what phrase can you use in Indonesian?**

   a) Saya ingin cokelat.
   b) Saya melihat kecelakaan.
   c) Saya suka bunga.
   d) Ini rumah saya.

8. **What's the Indonesian word for "help"?**

   a) Selamat tinggal
   b) Selamat siang
   c) Terima kasih
   d) Tolong!

9. **How would you say "I've been robbed; I need the authorities" in Indonesian?**

   a) Saya makan keju.
   b) Saya telah dirampok; saya membutuhkan bantuan pihak berwenang.
   c) Ini gunung yang indah.

10. **How do you ask "Can you call an ambulance, please?" in Indonesian?**

    a) Bisakah Anda memanggil taksi, tolong?
    b) Bisakah Anda memberi saya garam?
    c) Bisakah Anda memanggil ambulans, tolong?

11. What's the Indonesian word for "emergency services"?

a) Layanan Darurat
b) Kue lezat
c) Ringan

12. How do you say "reporting an accident" in Indonesian?

a) Menyanyi lagu
b) Membaca buku
c) Melaporkan kecelakaan

13. If you need to contact the fire department, what should you say in Indonesian?

a) Bagaimana cara saya ke perpustakaan?
b) Saya perlu menghubungi pemadam kebakaran.
c) Saya mencari teman saya.

14. What's the Indonesian word for "urgent"?

a) Kecil
b) Cantik
c) Cepat
d) Mendesak

15. How do you ask for the nearest police station in Indonesian?

a) Di mana toko roti terdekat?
b) Di mana kantor polisi terdekat?
c) Apakah Anda memiliki peta?
d) Jam berapa sekarang?

Correct Answers:

1. b)
2. c)
3. c)
4. c)
5. b)
6. c)
7. b)
8. d)
9. b)
10. c)
11. a)
12. c)
13. b)
14. d)
15. b)

EVERYDAY CONVERSATIONS

- SMALL TALK AND CASUAL CONVERSATIONS -
- DISCUSSING THE WEATHER, HOBBIES, AND INTERESTS -
- MAKING PLANS WITH FRIENDS OR ACQUAINTANCES -

Small Talk

438. How's it going?
Bagaimana kabarmu?
(Bah-gai-mah-nah kah-bahr-moo?)

439. Nice weather we're having, isn't it?
Cuacanya bagus, bukan?
(Choo-ah-chah-nyah bah-goos, boo-kahn?)

440. Have any exciting plans for the weekend?
Ada rencana menarik untuk akhir pekan?
(Ah-dah ren-chah-nah meh-nah-reek oon-took ahk-heer peh-kahn?)

441. Did you catch that new movie?
Sudah menonton film baru itu?
(Soo-dah meh-non-ton feelm bah-roo ee-too?)

442. How's your day been so far?
Bagaimana harimu sejauh ini?
(Bah-gai-mah-nah hah-ree-moo seh-jowh ee-nee?)

443. What do you do for work?
Kamu bekerja sebagai apa?
(Kah-moo beh-kehr-jah seh-bah-gai ah-pah?)

444. Do you come here often?
Kamu sering datang ke sini?
(Kah-moo seh-ring dah-tahng keh see-nee?)

445. Have you tried the food at this place before?
Sudah pernah mencoba makanan di tempat ini?
(Soo-dah pehr-nah men-cho-bah mah-kah-nahn dee tem-paht ee-nee?)

446. Any recommendations for things to do in town?
Ada rekomendasi untuk aktivitas di kota ini?
(Ah-dah reh-koh-men-dah-see oon-took ahk-tee-vee-tahs dee koh-tah ee-nee?)

447. Do you follow any sports teams?
Kamu mengikuti tim olahraga tertentu?
(Kah-moo meng-ee-koo-tee teem oh-lah-rah-gah tehr-ten-too?)

448. Have you traveled anywhere interesting lately?
Baru-baru ini pernah bepergian ke tempat menarik?
(Bah-roo bah-roo ee-nee pehr-nah beh-per-gee-ahn keh tem-paht meh-nah-reek?)

449. Do you enjoy cooking?
Kamu suka memasak?
(Kah-moo soo-kah meh-mah-sahk?)

Travel Story: On a culinary adventure in Padang, a chef described the region's rich cuisine as "Tak lapuk dek hujan, tak lekang dek panas," meaning "Neither decayed by rain nor faded by the sun," signifying its timeless appeal.

Casual Conversations

450. What's your favorite type of music?
Jenis musik favoritmu apa?
(Jeh-nees moo-seek fah-vo-reet-moo ah-pah?)

Fun Fact: Indonesian uses the Latin alphabet.

451. How do you like to spend your free time?
Bagaimana kamu menghabiskan waktu luangmu?
(Bah-gai-mah-nah kah-moo meng-hah-bees-kahn wahk-too loo-ahng-moo?)

452. Do you have any pets?
Apakah kamu punya hewan peliharaan?
(Ah-pah-kah kah-moo poon-yah hew-an pe-lee-hah-ra-ahn?)

453. Where did you grow up?
Di mana kamu tumbuh besar?
(Dee mah-nah kah-moo toom-boo beh-sar?)

454. What's your family like?
Bagaimana keluargamu?
(Bah-gai-mah-nah ke-loo-ar-gah-moo?)

455. Are you a morning person or a night owl?
Apakah kamu orang pagi atau malam?
(Ah-pah-kah kah-moo oh-rang pah-gee ah-tow mah-lahm?)

456. Do you prefer coffee or tea?
Kamu lebih suka kopi atau teh?
(Kah-moo leh-beeh soo-kah koh-pee ah-tow teh?)

457. Are you into any TV shows right now?
Apakah kamu sedang mengikuti acara TV?
(Ah-pah-kah kah-moo seh-dahng meng-ee-koo-tee ah-char-rah tee-vee?)

Idiomatic Expression: "Naik daun." -
Meaning: "Becoming popular."
(Literal translation: "Rising leaf.")

458. What's the last book you read?
Buku apa yang terakhir kamu baca?
(Boo-koo ah-pah yahng teh-rahk-heer kah-moo bah-chah?)

459. Do you like to travel?
Apakah kamu suka bepergian?
(Ah-pah-kah kah-moo soo-kah beh-per-gee-ahn?)

460. Are you a fan of outdoor activities?
Apakah kamu suka aktivitas di luar ruangan?
(Ah-pah-kah kah-moo soo-kah ak-tee-vee-tahs dee loo-ahr roo-ahn-gahn?)

461. How do you unwind after a long day?
Bagaimana kamu bersantai setelah hari yang panjang?
(Bah-gai-mah-nah kah-moo ber-sahn-tai seh-tell-ah hah-ree yahng pahn-jahng?)

Discussing the Weather

462. Can you believe this heat/cold?
Apakah kamu percaya panas/dingin ini?
(Ah-pah-kah kah-moo per-chah-yah pah-nas/deen-geen ee-nee?)

463. I heard it's going to rain all week.
Saya dengar akan hujan sepanjang minggu.
(Sah-yah deh-ngahr ah-kahn hoo-jahn seh-pahn-jahng meeng-goo.)

464. What's the temperature like today?
Bagaimana suhu hari ini?
(Bah-gai-mah-nah soo-hoo hah-ree ee-nee?)

465. Do you like sunny or cloudy days better?
Kamu lebih suka hari cerah atau berawan?
(Kah-moo leh-beeh soo-kah hah-ree cheh-rah ah-tow beh-rah-wahn?)

466. Have you ever seen a snowstorm like this?
Pernahkah kamu melihat badai salju seperti ini?
(Per-nah-kah kah-moo meh-lee-hat bah-dye sal-joo sep-er-tee ee-nee?)

467. Is it always this humid here?
Apakah selalu lembab seperti ini di sini?
(Ah-pah-kah seh-lah-loo lehm-bahb sep-er-tee ee-nee dee see-nee?)

468. Did you get caught in that thunderstorm yesterday?
Kemarin kamu terjebak dalam badai petir itu?
(Keh-mah-reen kah-moo ter-jeh-bahk dah-lahm bah-dye peh-teer ee-too?)

469. What's the weather like in your hometown?
Bagaimana cuaca di kampung halamanmu?
(Bah-gai-mah-nah chua-chah dee kahm-poong hah-lah-mahn-moo?)

470. I can't stand the wind; how about you?
Saya tidak tahan angin; bagaimana denganmu?
(Sah-yah tee-dahk tah-hahn ahn-geen; bah-gai-mah-nah dehng-ahn-moo?)

471. Is it true the winters here are mild?
Apakah benar musim dingin di sini lembut?
(Ah-pah-kah beh-nahr moo-seem deen-geen dee see-nee lehm-boot?)

472. Do you like beach weather?
Kamu suka cuaca pantai?
(*Kah-moo soo-kah chua-chah pahn-tie?)*

473. How do you cope with the humidity in summer?
Bagaimana kamu mengatasi kelembapan di musim panas?
(*Bah-gai-mah-nah kah-moo meng-ah-tah-see keh-lem-bah-pahn dee moo-seem pah-nahs?)*

Hobbies

474. What are your hobbies or interests?
Apa hobimu atau minatmu?
(*Ah-pah ho-bee-moo ah-tow mee-nah-t-moo?)*

475. Do you play any musical instruments?
Apakah kamu bermain alat musik?
(*Ah-pah-kah kah-moo ber-mine ah-lahht moo-seek?)*

476. Have you ever tried painting or drawing?
Pernahkah kamu mencoba melukis atau menggambar?
(*Per-nah-kah kah-moo men-cho-bah meh-loo-kees ah-tow meng-gahm-bar?)*

477. Are you a fan of sports?
Apakah kamu penggemar olahraga?
(*Ah-pah-kah kah-moo peng-geh-mar oh-lah-rah-gah?)*

478. Do you enjoy cooking or baking?
Apakah kamu suka memasak atau membuat kue?
(*Ah-pah-kah kah-moo soo-kah meh-mah-sahk ah-tow mehm-boo-at koo-eh?)*

479. Are you into photography?
Apakah kamu tertarik dengan fotografi?
(Ah-pah-kah kah-moo ter-tah-reek dehng-ahn foh-toh-grah-fee?)

480. Have you ever tried gardening?
Pernahkah kamu mencoba berkebun?
(Per-nah-kah kah-moo men-cho-bah ber-keh-boon?)

481. Do you like to read in your free time?
Apakah kamu suka membaca di waktu luangmu?
(Ah-pah-kah kah-moo soo-kah mem-bah-chah dee wahk-too loo-ahng-moo?)

482. Have you explored any new hobbies lately?
Belakangan ini, apakah kamu mengeksplorasi hobi baru?
(Beh-lah-kahn-gahn ee-nee, ah-pah-kah kah-moo meng-ek-splor-ah-see hoh-bee bah-roo?)

483. Are you a collector of anything?
Apakah kamu seorang kolektor sesuatu?
(Ah-pah-kah kah-moo seh-oh-rahng koh-lek-tor seh-soo-ah-too?)

484. Do you like to watch movies or TV shows?
Apakah kamu suka menonton film atau acara TV?
(Ah-pah-kah kah-moo soo-kah meh-non-ton feelm ah-tow ah-chah-rah tee-vee?)

485. Have you ever taken up a craft project?
Pernahkah kamu melakukan proyek kerajinan tangan?
(Per-nah-kah kah-moo meh-loo-ah-kahn pro-yek keh-rah-jee-nahn tahng-ahn?)

Idiomatic Expression: “Pagar makan tanaman.” - Meaning: "A betrayal by someone close." (Literal translation: "The fence eats the crops.")

Interests

486. What topics are you passionate about?
Topik apa yang kamu bersemangat tentang?
(Toh-peek ah-pah yahng kah-moo ber-seh-mahn-gaht ten-tahng?)

487. Are you involved in any social causes?
Apakah kamu terlibat dalam sebab-sebab sosial?
(Ah-pah-kah kah-moo ter-lee-baht dah-lahm seh-bahb-seh-bahb soh-syahhl?)

488. Do you enjoy learning new languages?
Apakah kamu menikmati belajar bahasa baru?
(Ah-pah-kah kah-moo meh-neek-mah-tee beh-lah-jahr bah-hah-sah bah-roo?)

489. Are you into fitness or wellness?
Apakah kamu tertarik dengan kebugaran atau kesehatan?
(Ah-pah-kah kah-moo ter-tah-reek dehng-ahn keh-boo-gah-rahn ah-tow keh-seh-hah-tahn?)

490. Are you a technology enthusiast?
Apakah kamu penggemar teknologi?
(Ah-pah-kah kah-moo peng-geh-mar tek-no-loh-gee?)

491. What's your favorite genre of books or movies?
Genre buku atau film apa yang paling kamu sukai?
(Jen-reh boo-koo ah-tow feelm ah-pah yahng pah-leeng kah-moo soo-kai?)

492. Do you follow current events or politics?
Apakah kamu mengikuti peristiwa terkini atau politik?
(Ah-pah-kah kah-moo meng-ee-koo-tee peh-rees-tee-wah ter-kee-nee ah-tow poh-lee-teek?)

493. Are you into fashion or design?
Apakah kamu tertarik dengan mode atau desain?
(Ah-pah-kah kah-moo ter-tah-reek dehng-ahn moh-deh ah-tow deh-sine?)

494. Are you a history buff?
Apakah kamu penggemar sejarah?
(Ah-pah-kah kah-moo peng-ge-mar seh-jah-rah?)

495. Have you ever been involved in volunteer work?
Pernahkah kamu terlibat dalam pekerjaan sukarela?
(Per-nah-kah kah-moo ter-lee-baht dah-lahm peh-ker-jah-ahn soo-kah-reh-lah?)

496. Are you passionate about cooking or food culture?
Apakah kamu bersemangat tentang memasak atau budaya makanan?
(Ah-pah-kah kah-moo ber-seh-mahn-gaht ten-tahng meh-mah-sak ah-tow boo-dah-yah mah-kah-nahn?)

497. Are you an advocate for any specific hobbies or interests?
Apakah kamu pendukung hobi atau minat tertentu?
(Ah-pah-kah kah-moo pen-doo-kung hoh-bee ah-tow mee-naht ter-ten-too?)

Idiomatic Expression: “Pisau cukur.” -
Meaning: "Someone who is very sharp or cunning."
(Literal translation: "Razor blade.")

Making Plans

498. Would you like to grab a coffee sometime?
Apakah kamu ingin minum kopi suatu saat?
(Ah-pah-kah kah-moo een-geen mee-noom koh-pee soo-ah-too sah-aht?)

499. Let's plan a dinner outing this weekend.
Mari merencanakan makan malam akhir pekan ini.
(Mah-ree meh-ren-cha-nah-kahn mah-kahn mah-lahm ahk-heer peh-kahn ee-nee.)

500. How about going to a movie on Friday night?
Bagaimana dengan menonton film pada malam Jumat?
(Bah-guy-mah-nah dehng-ahn meh-non-ton feelm pah-dah mah-lahm Joo-maht?)

501. Do you want to join us for a hike next weekend?
Apakah kamu ingin bergabung dengan kami untuk mendaki akhir pekan depan?
(Ah-pah-kah kah-moo een-geen ber-gah-boong dehng-ahn kah-mee oon-took men-dah-kee ahk-heer peh-kahn deh-pahn?)

502. We should organize a game night soon.
Kita harus mengadakan malam permainan segera.
(Kee-tah hah-roos meng-ah-dah-kahn mah-lahm per-mai-nahn seh-geh-rah.)

503. Let's catch up over lunch next week.
Mari bertemu dan ngobrol saat makan siang minggu depan.
(Mah-ree ber-teh-moo dahn ngo-brol sah-aht mah-kahn see-ahng ming-goo deh-pahn.)

504. Would you be interested in a shopping trip?
Apakah kamu tertarik untuk pergi belanja?
(Ah-pah-kah kah-moo ter-tah-reek oon-took per-gee be-lahn-jah?)

505. I'm thinking of visiting the museum; care to join?
Saya berpikir untuk mengunjungi museum; ingin bergabung?
(Sah-yah ber-peek-eer oon-took meng-oon-joong-ee moo-seh-um; een-geen ber-gah-boong?)

506. How about a picnic in the park?
Bagaimana dengan piknik di taman?
(Bah-guy-mah-nah dehng-ahn peek-neek dee tah-mahn?)

> **Fun Fact:** Indonesia has Southeast Asia's largest economy.

507. Let's get together for a study session.
Mari kumpul untuk sesi belajar.
(Mah-ree koom-pool oon-took seh-see be-lah-jar.)

508. We should plan a beach day this summer.
Kita harus merencanakan hari di pantai musim panas ini.
(Kee-tah hah-roos meh-ren-cha-nah-kahn hah-ree dee pahn-tie moo-seem pah-nahs ee-nee.)

509. Want to come over for a barbecue at my place?
Mau datang ke tempatku untuk barbeku?
(Mow dah-tahng keh tem-paht-koo oon-took bar-be-koo?)

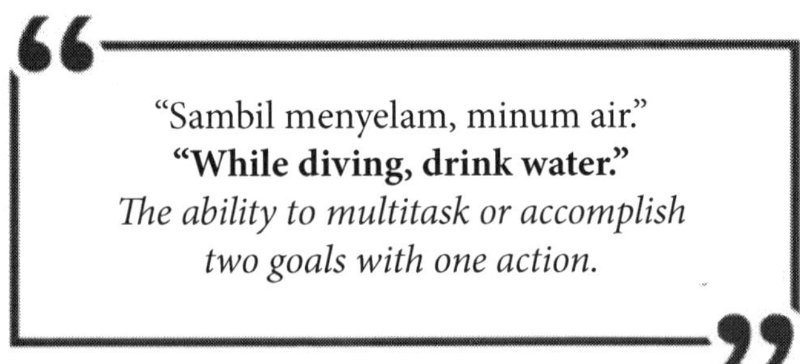

Interactive Challenge: Everyday Conversations

(Link each English word with their corresponding meaning in Indonesian)

1) Conversation	Komunikasi
2) Greeting	Dialog
3) Question	Salam
4) Answer	Percakapan Santai
5) Salutation	Ekspresi
6) Communication	Berbagi Ide
7) Dialogue	Jawaban
8) Small Talk	Bahasa
9) Discussion	Tukar Pendapat
10) Speech	Obrolan Ringan
11) Language	Diskusi
12) Exchange of Opinions	Percakapan
13) Expression	Pidato
14) Casual Conversation	Pertanyaan
15) Sharing Ideas	Sapaan

Correct Answers:

1. Conversation - Percakapan
2. Greeting - Salam
3. Question - Pertanyaan
4. Answer - Jawaban
5. Salutation - Sapaan
6. Communication - Komunikasi
7. Dialogue - Dialog
8. Small Talk - Obrolan Ringan
9. Discussion - Diskusi
10. Speech - Pidato
11. Language - Bahasa
12. Exchange of Opinions - Tukar Pendapat
13. Expression - Ekspresi
14. Casual Conversation - Percakapan Santai
15. Sharing Ideas - Berbagi Ide

BUSINESS & WORK

- INTRODUCING YOURSELF IN A PROFESSIONAL SETTING -
- DISCUSSING WORK-RELATED TOPICS -
- NEGOTIATING BUSINESS DEALS OR CONTRACTS -

Professional Introductions

510. Hi, I'm [Your Name].
Hai, saya [Nama Anda].
(Hi, sah-yah [Nah-mah Ahn-dah].)

511. What do you do for a living?
Apa pekerjaan Anda?
(Ah-pah peh-ker-jah-an Ahn-dah?)

512. What's your role in the company?
Apa peran Anda di perusahaan?
(Ah-pah peh-rahn Ahn-dah dee peh-roo-sah-hahn?)

513. Can you tell me about your background?
Bisa ceritakan tentang latar belakang Anda?
(Bee-sah cheh-ree-tah-kahn ten-tahng lah-tahr beh-lah-kahng Ahn-dah?)

514. This is my colleague, [Colleague's Name].
Ini rekan kerja saya, [Nama Rekan Kerja].
(Ee-nee reh-kahn ker-jah sah-yah, [Nah-mah Reh-kahn Ker-jah].)

515. May I introduce myself?
Bolehkah saya memperkenalkan diri?
(Boh-leh-kah sah-yah mem-per-ken-al-kan dee-ree?)

516. I work in [Your Department].
Saya bekerja di [Departemen Anda].
(Sah-yah beh-ker-jah dee [Deh-pahr-teh-men Ahn-dah].)

517. How long have you been with the company?
Sudah berapa lama Anda bekerja di perusahaan ini?
(Soo-dah beh-rah-pah lah-mah Ahn-dah beh-ker-jah dee peh-roo-sah-hahn ee-nee?)

518. Are you familiar with our team?
Apakah Anda sudah familiar dengan tim kami?
(Ah-pah-kah Ahn-dah soo-dah fah-mee-lee-ahr dehng-ahn teem kah-mee?)

519. Let me introduce you to our manager.
Izinkan saya memperkenalkan Anda kepada manajer kami.
(Ee-zeen-kahn sah-yah mem-per-ken-al-kan Ahn-dah keh-pah-dah mah-nah-jehr kah-mee.)

> **Travel Story:** In a traditional puppet show in Central Java, the puppeteer used the phrase "Seperti kacang lupa kulit," to describe a character who had forgotten his roots.

Work Conversations

520. Can we discuss the project?
Bisa kita bahas proyek ini?
(Bee-sah kee-tah bah-hahs pro-yek ee-nee?)

521. Let's go over the details.
Mari kita ulas detailnya.
(Mah-ree kee-tah oo-lahs deh-tail-nyah.)

522. What's the agenda for the meeting?
Apa agenda untuk rapat ini?
(Ah-pah ah-jen-dah oon-took rah-paht ee-nee?)

523. I'd like your input on this.
Saya ingin mendengar pendapat Anda tentang ini.
(Sah-yah een-geen men-deng-ar pen-dah-paht Ahn-dah ten-tahng ee-nee.)

524. We need to address this issue.
Kita perlu menangani masalah ini.
(Kee-tah pehr-loo meh-nahn-gee mah-sah-lah ee-nee.)

525. How's the project progressing?
Bagaimana kemajuan proyek?
(Bah-gah-ee-mah-nah keh-mah-juan pro-yek?)

526. Do you have any updates for me?
Ada pembaruan untuk saya?
(Ah-dah pem-bah-roo-ahn oon-took sah-yah?)

527. Let's brainstorm some ideas.
Mari kita curahkan beberapa ide.
(Mah-ree kee-tah coor-rahk-kan beh-buh-rah ee-deh.)

528. Can we schedule a team meeting?
Bisa kita jadwalkan pertemuan tim?
(Bee-sah kee-tah jahd-wahl-kahn pehr-te-moo-ahn teem?)

529. I'm open to suggestions.
Saya terbuka untuk saran.
(Sah-yah tehr-boo-kah oon-took sah-rahn.)

Business Negotiations

530. We need to negotiate the terms.
Kita perlu menegosiasikan syarat-syarat.
(Kee-tah pehr-loo meh-neh-goh-see-ah-see-kahn sya-raht-sya-raht.)

531. What's your offer?
Apa tawaran Anda?
(Ah-pah tah-wah-rahn Ahn-dah?)

532. Can we find a middle ground?
Bisakah kita menemukan jalan tengah?
(Bee-sah-kah kee-tah meh-ne-moo-kahn jah-lahn teng-gah?)

Idiomatic Expression: "Pasang telinga." -
Meaning: "To listen attentively."
(Literal translation: "Install the ear.")

533. Let's discuss the contract.
Mari kita diskusikan kontrak.
(Mah-ree kee-tah dees-koo-see-kahn kohn-trahk.)

534. Are you flexible on the price?
Apakah Anda fleksibel dengan harga?
(Ah-pah-kah Ahn-dah flek-see-bel dehng-ahn hahr-gah?)

535. I'd like to propose a deal.
Saya ingin mengusulkan kesepakatan.
(Sah-yah een-geen mehng-oo-sool-kahn keh-seh-pah-kah-tahn.)

536. We're interested in your terms.
Kami tertarik dengan syarat-syarat Anda.
(Kah-mee tehr-tah-reek dehng-ahn sya-raht-sya-raht Ahn-dah.)

537. Can we talk about the agreement?
Bisakah kita berbicara tentang perjanjian?
(Bee-sah-kah kee-tah behr-bee-chah-rah ten-tahng pehr-jahn-jee-ahn?)

Fun Fact: Indonesian is a gender-neutral language.

538. Let's work out the details.
Mari kita atur detailnya.
(Mah-ree kee-tah ah-toor deh-tail-nyah.)

539. What are your conditions?
Apa syarat-syarat Anda?
(Ah-pah sya-raht-sya-raht Ahn-dah?)

540. We should reach a compromise.
Kita harus mencapai kompromi.
(Kee-tah hah-roos men-cha-pie kom-pro-mee.)

Fun Fact: Some ethnic groups, like the Minangkabau, are matrilineal.

Workplace Etiquette

541. Remember to be punctual.
Ingatlah untuk tepat waktu.
(Eeng-aht-lah oon-took teh-paht wah-ktoo.)

542. Always maintain a professional demeanor.
Selalu jaga sikap profesional.
(Seh-lah-loo jah-gah see-kap pro-fe-syon-al.)

543. Respect your colleagues' personal space.
Hormati ruang pribadi rekan kerja Anda.
(Hor-mah-tee roo-ahng pree-bah-dee reh-kahn ker-jah Ahn-dah.)

Fun Fact: Indonesia is famous for its diverse textile arts, including Ikat and Songket.

544. Dress appropriately for the office.
Berpakaianlah yang sesuai untuk kantor.
(Berr-pah-kai-yahn-lah yahng seh-soo-eye oon-took kahn-tor.)

545. Follow company policies and guidelines.
Ikuti kebijakan dan pedoman perusahaan.
(Ee-koo-tee keh-bee-jah-kahn dahn peh-doh-mahn peh-roo-shah-ahn.)

546. Use respectful language in conversations.
Gunakan bahasa yang sopan dalam percakapan.
(Goo-nah-kahn bah-sah yahng soh-pahn dahl-am pehr-chah-kah-pahn.)

547. Keep your workspace organized.
Jaga kebersihan ruang kerja Anda.
(Jah-gah keh-berr-see-hahn roo-ahng ker-jah Ahn-dah.)

548. Be mindful of office noise levels.
Perhatikan tingkat kebisingan kantor.
(Per-hah-tee-kahn teeng-kaht keh-bee-sing-gahn kahn-tor.)

549. Offer assistance when needed.
Tawarkan bantuan jika diperlukan.
(Tah-war-kahn bahn-too-ahn jee-kah dee-per-loo-kahn.)

550. Practice good hygiene at work.
Praktikkan kebersihan baik di tempat kerja.
(Prahk-teek-kahn keh-berr-see-hahn baik dee tem-paht ker-jah.)

551. Avoid office gossip and rumors.
Hindari gosip dan rumor di kantor.
(Hin-dah-ree goh-sip dahn roo-mor dee kahn-tor.)

Job Interviews

552. Tell me about yourself.
Ceritakan tentang dirimu.
(Che-ree-tah-kahn ten-tahng dee-ree-moo.)

553. What are your strengths and weaknesses?
Apa kekuatan dan kelemahanmu?
(Ah-pah keh-koo-ah-tahn dahn keh-leh-mah-hahn-moo?)

554. Describe your relevant experience.
Jelaskan pengalaman relevanmu.
(Jeh-lahs-kahn peng-ah-lah-man reh-leh-vahn-moo.)

555. Why do you want to work here?
Mengapa kamu ingin bekerja di sini?
(Meng-ah-pah kah-moo een-geen beh-ker-jah dee see-nee?)

556. Where do you see yourself in five years?
Kamu melihat dirimu di mana dalam lima tahun?
(Kah-moo meh-lee-aht dee-ree-moo dee mah-nah dah-lahm lee-mah tah-oon?)

557. How do you handle challenges at work?
Bagaimana kamu mengatasi tantangan di pekerjaan?
(Bah-guy-mah-nah kah-moo meng-ah-tah-see tahn-tahn-gahn dee peh-ker-jah-ahn?)

558. What interests you about this position?
Apa yang menarikmu tentang posisi ini?
(Ah-pah yahng meh-nah-reek-moo ten-tahng poh-see-see ee-nee?)

559. Can you provide an example of your teamwork?
Bisa memberikan contoh kerjasama timmu?
(Bee-sah mehm-beh-ree-kahn kon-toh ker-jah-sah-mah teem-moo?)

560. What motivates you in your career?
Apa yang memotivasimu dalam karirmu?
(Ah-pah yahng meh-moh-tee-vah-see-moo dah-lahm kah-reer-moo?)

561. Do you have any questions for us?
Ada pertanyaan untuk kami?
(Ah-dah per-tahn-yah-ahn oon-took kah-mee?)

562. Thank you for considering me for the role.
Terima kasih telah mempertimbangkan saya untuk peran ini.
(Teh-ree-mah kah-see te-lah mem-per-tim-bang-kahn sah-yah oon-took peh-rahn ee-nee.)

Office Communication

563. Send me an email about it.
Kirimkan saya email tentang itu.
(Kee-reem-kahn sah-yah e-may-el ten-tahng ee-too.)

564. Let's schedule a conference call.
Mari kita jadwalkan panggilan konferensi.
(Mah-ree kee-tah jahd-wahl-kahn pahng-gee-lahn kon-feh-ren-see.)

565. Could you clarify your message?
Bisa menjelaskan pesanmu?
(Bee-sah men-jeh-lahs-kahn peh-sahn-moo?)

566. I'll forward the document to you.
Aku akan meneruskan dokumen itu kepadamu.
(Ah-koo ah-kahn meh-neh-roos-kahn doh-koo-men ee-too keh-pah-dah-moo.)

567. Please reply to this message.
Tolong balas pesan ini.
(Toh-long bah-lahs peh-sahn ee-nee.)

568. We should have a team meeting.
Kita harus mengadakan rapat tim.
(Kee-tah hah-roos meng-ah-dah-kahn rah-paht teem.)

> **Idiomatic Expression:** "Seperti kucing kurap." - Meaning: "Insignificant."
> (Literal translation: "Like a mangy cat.")

569. Check your inbox for updates.
Periksa kotak masukmu untuk pembaruan.
(Peh-reek-sah koh-tahk mah-sook-moo oon-took pem-bah-roo-ahn.)

570. I'll copy you on the correspondence.
Aku akan menyalinmu dalam korespondensi.
(Ah-koo ah-kahn meh-nyah-leen-moo dah-lahm koh-res-pon-den-see.)

571. I'll send you the meeting agenda.
Aku akan mengirimkanmu agenda rapat.
(Ah-koo ah-kahn meng-ee-reem-kahn-moo ah-jen-dah rah-paht.)

572. Use the internal messaging system.
Gunakan sistem pesan internal.
(Goo-nah-kahn see-stem peh-sahn in-ter-nahl.)

573. Keep everyone in the loop.
Pastikan semua orang dalam lingkaran informasi.
(*Pahs-tee-kahn seh-moo-ah oh-rahng dah-lahm leeng-kah-rahn in-for-mah-see.*)

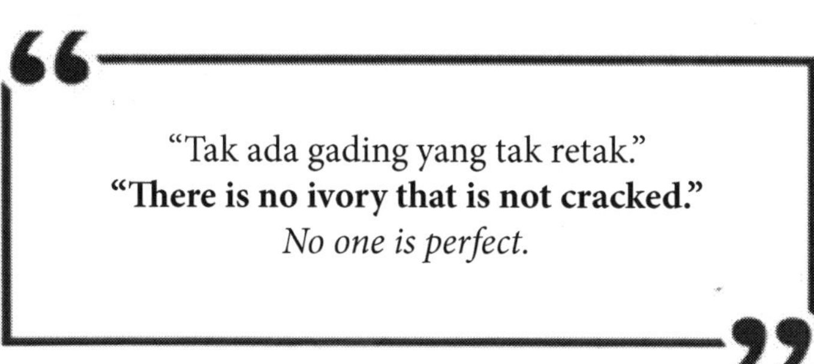

Cross Word Puzzle: Business & Work

(Provide the Indonesian translation for the following English words)

Across

2. - BOSS
6. - PROFESSIONAL
8. - SALARY
9. - CONTRACT
11. - WORK
13. - TEAM

Down

1. - BUSINESS
3. - INCOME
4. - PRODUCT
5. - SERVICE
6. - MARKETING
7. - CLIENT
10. - PROJECT
11. - EMPLOYEE
12. - OFFICE

Correct Answers:

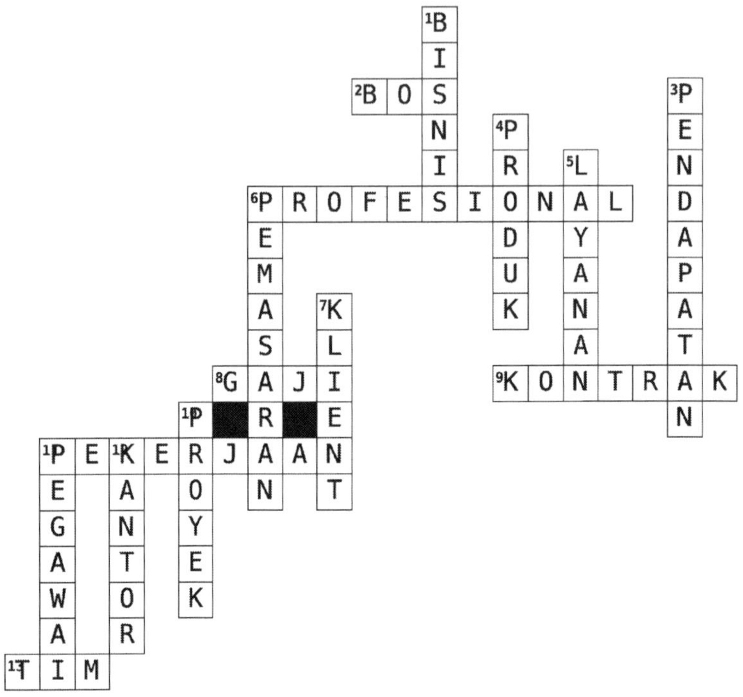

EVENTS & ENTERTAINMENT

- BUYING TICKETS FOR CONCERTS, MOVIES OR EVENTS -
- DISCUSSING ENTERTAINMENT & LEISURE ACTIVITIES -
- EXPRESSING JOY OR DISAPPOINTMENT WITH AN EVENT -

Ticket Purchases

574. I'd like to buy two tickets for the concert.
Saya ingin membeli dua tiket untuk konser.
(Sah-yah in-geen mem-beh-lee doo-ah tee-ket oon-took kon-ser.)

575. Can I get tickets for the movie tonight?
Bisa saya mendapatkan tiket untuk film malam ini?
(Bee-sah sah-yah men-dah-pah-tah-kan tee-ket oon-took feelm mah-lahm ee-nee?)

576. We need to book tickets for the upcoming event.
Kami perlu memesan tiket untuk acara mendatang.
(Kah-mee per-loo meh-meh-sahn tee-ket oon-took ah-chah-rah men-dah-tahng.)

577. What's the price of admission?
Berapa harga masuknya?
(Beh-rah-pah hahr-gah mah-sook-nyah?)

578. Do you offer any discounts for students?
Apakah ada diskon untuk pelajar?
(Ah-pah-kah ah-dah dis-kon oon-took peh-lah-jahr?)

579. Are there any available seats for the matinee?
Apakah ada tempat duduk yang tersedia untuk matine?
(Ah-pah-kah ah-dah tem-paht doo-dook yahng ter-seh-dee-ah oon-took mah-tee-neh?)

580. How can I purchase tickets online?
Bagaimana saya bisa membeli tiket secara online?
(Bah-gah-ee-mah-nah sah-yah bee-sah mem-beh-lee tee-ket se-kah-rah on-line?)

581. Is there a box office nearby?
Apakah ada loket tiket di dekat sini?
(*Ah-pah-kah ah-dah loh-ket tee-ket dee deh-kaht see-nee?)*

582. Are tickets refundable if I can't attend?
Apakah tiket bisa dikembalikan jika saya tidak bisa hadir?
(Ah-pah-kah tee-ket bee-sah dee-kem-bah-lee-kahn jee-kah sah-yah tee-dahk bee-sah hah-deer?)

583. Can I choose my seats for the show?
Bisakah saya memilih kursi saya untuk pertunjukan?
(Bee-sah-kah sah-yah meh-mee-leeh koor-see sah-yah oon-took per-toon-joo-kahn?)

584. Can I reserve tickets for the theater?
Bisakah saya memesan tiket untuk teater?
(*Bee-sah-kah sah-yah meh-meh-sahn tee-ket oon-took teh-ah-ter?)*

585. How early should I buy event tickets?
Seberapa awal saya harus membeli tiket acara?
(Seh-beh-rah-pah ah-wahl sah-yah hah-roos mem-beh-lee tee-ket ah-chah-rah?)

586. Are there any VIP packages available?
Apakah ada paket VIP yang tersedia?
(Ah-pah-kah ah-dah pah-ket Vee-ee-peh yahng ter-seh-dee-ah?)

587. What's the seating arrangement like?
Bagaimana susunan tempat duduknya?
(Bah-gah-ee-mah-nah soo-soo-nahn tem-paht doo-dook-nyah?)

Idiomatic Expression: "Sudah jatuh tertimpa tangga." - Meaning: "When things go from bad to worse." (Literal translation: "Already fallen, then hit by a ladder.")

588. Is there a family discount for the movie?
Apakah ada diskon keluarga untuk film ini?
(Ah-pah-kah ah-dah dis-kon ke-loo-ar-gah oon-took feel-eem ee-nee?)

589. I'd like to purchase tickets for my friends.
Saya ingin membeli tiket untuk teman-teman saya.
(Sah-yah in-geen mem-beh-lee tee-ket oon-took teh-mahn-teh-mahn sah-yah.)

Fun Fact: Indonesia is a major rice-producing country.

590. Do they accept credit cards for tickets?
Apakah mereka menerima kartu kredit untuk tiket?
(Ah-pah-kah meh-reh-kah meh-nehr-mah kar-too kreh-deet oon-took tee-ket?)

591. Are there any age restrictions for entry?
Apakah ada batasan usia untuk masuk?
(Ah-pah-kah ah-dah bah-tah-sahn oo-see-ah oon-took mah-sook?)

592. Can I exchange my ticket for a different date?
Bisakah saya menukar tiket saya dengan tanggal yang berbeda?
(Bee-sah-kah sah-yah meh-noo-kar tee-ket sah-yah dehng-an tahn-gahl yahng ber-beh-dah?)

Leisure Activities

593. What do you feel like doing this weekend?
Apa yang ingin kamu lakukan di akhir pekan ini?
(Ah-pah yahng in-geen kah-moo lah-koo-kahn dee ahk-heer peh-kahn ee-nee?)

594. Let's discuss our entertainment options.
Mari kita membahas pilihan hiburan kita.
(Mah-ree kee-tah mem-bah-hahs pee-lee-hahn hee-boo-ran kee-tah.)

> **Fun Fact:** Jakarta has one of the world's most extensive bus rapid transit systems.

595. I'm planning a leisurely hike on Saturday.
Saya merencanakan pendakian santai pada hari Sabtu.
(Sah-yah meh-ren-chah-nah-kahn pen-dah-kee-ahn san-tie pah-dah hah-ree Sahb-too.)

596. Do you enjoy outdoor activities like hiking?
Apakah kamu menikmati aktivitas luar ruang seperti mendaki?
(Ah-pah-kah kah-moo meh-neek-mah-tee ak-tee-vee-tahs loo-ar roo-ahng se-per-tee men-dah-kee?)

597. Have you ever tried indoor rock climbing?
Pernahkah kamu mencoba panjat tebing dalam ruangan?
(Per-nah-kah kah-moo men-cho-bah pan-jat teh-bing dah-lahm roo-ahng-gahn?)

598. I'd like to explore some new hobbies.
Saya ingin mengeksplorasi hobi-hobi baru.
(Sah-yah in-geen men-gek-splor-ah-see hoh-bee-hoh-bee bah-roo.)

599. What are your favorite pastimes?
Apa kegiatan favoritmu?
(Ah-pah keh-gee-ah-tahn fah-vo-reet-moo?)

> **Cultural Insight:** Family and communal ties are paramount in Indonesian society, often influencing personal and business relations.

600. Are there any interesting events in town?
Apakah ada acara menarik di kota?
(Ah-pah-kah ah-dah ah-cha-rah meh-nah-reek dee koh-tah?)

601. Let's check out the local art exhibition.
Mari kita lihat pameran seni lokal.
(Mah-ree kee-tah lee-haht pah-meh-rahn seh-nee loh-kahl.)

602. How about attending a cooking class?
Bagaimana dengan mengikuti kelas memasak?
(Bah-guy-mah-nah dehng-an meng-ee-koo-tee keh-lahs meh-mah-sahk?)

603. Let's explore some new recreational activities.
Mari kita jelajahi aktivitas rekreasi baru.
(Mah-ree kee-tah jeh-lah-hee ak-tee-vee-tahs reh-kreh-ah-see bah-roo.)

604. What's your go-to leisure pursuit?
Apa kegiatan santai favoritmu?
(Ah-pah keh-gee-ah-tahn sahn-tie fah-voh-reet-moo?)

605. I'm considering trying a new hobby.
Saya mempertimbangkan untuk mencoba hobi baru.
(Sah-yah mehm-per-teen-bahng-kahn oon-took men-cho-bah hoh-bee bah-roo.)

606. Have you ever attended a painting workshop?
Pernahkah kamu menghadiri workshop melukis?
(Per-nah-kah kah-moo meng-hah-dee-ree wor-shop meh-loo-kees?)

Fun Fact: National Language Day is celebrated on October 28th, marking the youth pledge of 1928.

607. What's your favorite way to unwind?
Apa cara favoritmu untuk bersantai?
(Ah-pah chah-rah fah-voh-reet-moo oon-took ber-sahn-tie?)

608. I'm interested in joining a local club.
Saya tertarik bergabung dengan klub lokal.
(Sah-yah ter-tah-reek ber-gah-boong dehng-an kloob loh-kahl.)

609. Let's plan a day filled with leisure.
Mari kita rencanakan hari yang penuh dengan kegiatan santai.
(Mah-ree kee-tah ren-cha-nah-kahn hah-ree yahng peh-noo dehng-an keh-gee-ah-tahn sahn-tie.)

610. Have you ever been to a live comedy show?
Pernahkah kamu ke pertunjukan komedi langsung?
(Per-nah-kah kah-moo keh per-toon-joo-kahn koh-meh-dee lahng-soong?)

611. I'd like to attend a cooking demonstration.
Saya ingin menghadiri demonstrasi memasak.
(Sah-yah een-geen meng-hah-dee-ree deh-mon-strah-see meh-mah-sahk.)

Fun Fact: Historically, the Maluku Islands were known as the Spice Islands.

Event Reactions

612. That concert was amazing! I loved it!
Konser itu luar biasa! Saya sangat menyukainya!
(Kon-ser ee-too loo-ahr bee-ah-sah! Sah-yah sahng-aht men-yoo-kie-nyah!)

613. I had such a great time at the movie.
Saya sangat menikmati waktu saya di film itu.
(Sah-yah sahng-aht meh-nee-kmah-tee wah-ktoo sah-yah dee feelm ee-too.)

614. The event exceeded my expectations.
Acara tersebut melampaui ekspektasi saya.
(Ah-cah-rah ter-seh-boo-ut meh-lam-pow-ee eks-pek-tah-see sah-yah.)

615. I was thrilled by the performance.
Saya sangat terkesan dengan penampilannya.
(Sah-yah sahng-aht ter-keh-san dehng-an peh-nam-peel-an-nya.)

616. It was an unforgettable experience.
Itu adalah pengalaman yang tak terlupakan.
(Ee-too ah-dah-lah peng-ah-lah-man yahng tahk ter-loo-pah-kan.)

617. I can't stop thinking about that show.
Saya tidak bisa berhenti memikirkan acara itu.
(Sah-yah tee-dahk bee-sah ber-hen-tee meh-mee-keer-kan ah-cah-rah ee-too.)

618. Unfortunately, the event was a letdown.
Sayangnya, acara tersebut mengecewakan.
(Sah-yang-nya, ah-cah-rah ter-seh-boo-ut men-geh-che-wah-kan.)

619. I was disappointed with the movie.
Saya kecewa dengan film itu.
(Sah-yah keh-che-wah dehng-an feelm ee-too.)

620. The concert didn't meet my expectations.
Konser itu tidak memenuhi ekspektasi saya.
(Kon-ser ee-too tee-dahk meh-me-noo-hee eks-pek-tah-see sah-yah.)

621. I expected more from the exhibition.
Saya mengharapkan lebih dari pameran itu.
(Sah-yah mehng-hah-rap-kan leh-beeh dah-ree pah-meh-ran ee-too.)

622. The event left me speechless; it was superb!
Acara itu membuat saya tak bisa berkata-kata; sungguh luar biasa!
(Ah-cah-rah ee-too mehm-boo-aht sah-yah tahk bee-sah ber-kah-tah-kah-tah; soong-goo loo-ar bee-ah-sah!)

623. I was absolutely thrilled with the performance.
Saya benar-benar terkesan dengan penampilannya.
(Sah-yah beh-nar-beh-nar ter-keh-san dehng-an peh-nam-peel-an-nya.)

624. The movie was a pleasant surprise.
Film itu adalah kejutan yang menyenangkan.
(Feel-eem ee-too ah-dah-lah keh-joo-tahn yahng meh-nyen-ang-kan.)

625. I had such a blast at the exhibition.
Saya sangat menikmati waktu di pameran itu.
(Sah-yah sahng-aht meh-nee-kmah-tee wah-ktoo dee pah-meh-ran ee-too.)

626. The concert was nothing short of fantastic.
Konser itu benar-benar fantastis.
(Kon-ser ee-too beh-nar-beh-nar fan-tas-tis.)

627. I'm still on cloud nine after the event.
Saya masih sangat bahagia setelah acara itu.
(Sah-yah mah-seeh sahng-aht bah-hah-gee-ah seh-teh-lah ah-cah-rah ee-too.)

628. I was quite underwhelmed by the show.
Saya cukup kecewa dengan pertunjukannya.
(*Sah-yah choo-koop keh-che-wah dehng-an per-toon-joohk-an-nya.)*

629. I expected more from the movie.
Saya mengharapkan lebih dari film tersebut.
(Sah-yah mehng-hah-rap-kahn leh-beeh dah-ree feelm ter-seh-boo-at.)

630. Unfortunately, the exhibition didn't impress me.
Sayangnya, pameran itu tidak membuat saya terkesan.
(Sah-yang-nya, pah-meh-rahn ee-too tee-dahk mehm-boo-at sah-yah ter-keh-san.)

"Bersatu kita teguh, bercerai kita runtuh."
"United we stand, divided we fall."
The importance of unity and teamwork.

Mini Lesson:
Basic Grammar Principles in Indonesian #2

Introduction:

Welcome to the second installment of our Indonesian grammar series. Expanding your understanding of Indonesian grammar is key to mastering both spoken and written forms of this fascinating language. In this lesson, we'll delve deeper into sentence structure, verb forms, and other essential elements of Indonesian grammar.

1. Sentence Structure:

Indonesian typically follows a Subject-Verb-Object (SVO) sentence structure, similar to English. However, the flexibility of Indonesian grammar allows for variations without changing the meaning.

- *Saya makan nasi. (I eat rice.)*
- *Makan saya nasi. (Eat I rice. [Still means "I eat rice."])*

2. Verb Forms:

Indonesian verbs do not conjugate based on tense or subject. Instead, time is indicated through time-specific words or context.

- *Saya makan kemarin. (I ate yesterday.)*
- *Saya akan makan. (I will eat.)*

3. Active and Passive Voice:

The passive voice is commonly used in Indonesian and is formed using the prefix "di-" or the word "oleh" for clarity.

- *Buku itu dibaca oleh siswa. (The book is read by the student.)*
- *Rumah itu dibangun tahun 1990. (The house was built in 1990.)*

4. Prefixes and Suffixes:

Indonesian extensively uses prefixes and suffixes to alter the meaning of root words, often changing nouns into verbs, and vice versa.

- *Baca (read) -> Membaca (to read)*
- *Tulis (write) -> Menulis (to write)*

5. Conditional Sentences:

Conditional sentences in Indonesian often use "jika" (if) or "kalau" (if/when).

- *Jika saya punya waktu, saya akan datang. (If I have time, I will come.)*
- *Kalau hujan, kita di rumah saja. (If it rains, we stay at home.)*

6. Adjectives:

Adjectives in Indonesian typically follow the noun they describe and do not change form.

- *Mobil merah (a red car)*
- *Buku tebal (a thick book)*

7. Demonstrative Pronouns:

Indonesian uses demonstrative pronouns like "ini" (this) and "itu" (that) to point out specific objects.

- *Buku ini bagus. (This book is good.)*
- *Rumah itu besar. (That house is big.)*

Conclusion:

Understanding these aspects of Indonesian grammar will enhance your language skills and help you communicate more effectively. Practice is essential, so immerse yourself in the language through conversations, media, and reading. Selamat belajar! (Happy learning!)

HEALTHCARE & MEDICAL NEEDS

- EXPLAINING SYMPTOMS TO A DOCTOR -
- REQUESTING MEDICAL ASSISTANCE -
- DISCUSSING MEDICATIONS AND TREATMENT -

Explaining Symptoms

631. I have a persistent headache.
Saya memiliki sakit kepala yang berkelanjutan.
(Sah-yah meh-meel-ee-kee sah-keet keh-pah-lah yahng ber-keh-lan-joo-tahn.)

632. My throat has been sore for a week.
Tenggorokan saya sudah sakit selama seminggu.
(Teng-goh-roh-kahn sah-yah soo-dah sah-keet seh-lah-mah seh-ming-goo.)

633. I've been experiencing stomach pain and nausea.
Saya mengalami sakit perut dan mual.
(Sah-yah meng-ah-lah-mee sah-keet peh-root dahn moo-ahl.)

634. I have a high fever and chills.
Saya memiliki demam tinggi dan menggigil.
(Sah-yah meh-meel-ee-kee deh-mahm teeng-gee dahn meng-gee-geel.)

635. My back has been hurting for a few days.
Punggung saya sudah sakit beberapa hari.
(Poong-goong sah-yah soo-dah sah-keet beh-beh-rah-pah hah-ree.)

636. I'm coughing up yellow mucus.
Saya batuk mengeluarkan lendir kuning.
(Sah-yah bah-took meng-eh-loo-ahr-kahn len-deer koo-neeng.)

637. I have a rash on my arm.
Saya memiliki ruam di lengan saya.
(Sah-yah meh-meel-ee-kee roo-ahm dee leng-gahn sah-yah.)

638. I've been having trouble breathing.
Saya kesulitan bernapas.
(Sah-yah keh-soo-lee-tahn ber-nah-pahs.)

639. I feel dizzy and lightheaded.
Saya merasa pusing dan ringan kepala.
(Sah-yah meh-rah-sah poo-seeng dahn reeng-gahn keh-pah-lah.)

640. My joints are swollen and painful.
Sendi-sendi saya bengkak dan sakit.
(Sen-dee sen-dee sah-yah beng-kahk dahn sah-keet.)

641. I've had diarrhea for two days.
Saya mengalami diare selama dua hari.
(Sah-yah meng-ah-lah-mee dee-ah-reh seh-lah-mah doo-ah hah-ree.)

642. My eyes are red and itchy.
Mata saya merah dan gatal.
(Mah-tah sah-yah meh-rah dahn gah-tahl.)

643. I've been vomiting since last night.
Saya muntah sejak semalam.
(Sah-yah moon-tah seh-jahk seh-mah-lahm.)

644. I have a painful, persistent toothache.
Saya memiliki sakit gigi yang berkelanjutan dan menyakitkan.
(Sah-yah meh-meel-ee-kee sah-keet gee-gee yahng ber-keh-lan-joo-tahn dahn meh-nyah-keet-kahn.)

645. I'm experiencing fatigue and weakness.
Saya merasakan kelelahan dan kelemahan.
(Sah-yah meh-rah-sah-kahn keh-leh-lah-hahn dahn keh-leh-mah hahn.)

646. I've noticed blood in my urine.
Saya memperhatikan darah dalam urin saya.
(*Sah-yah mem-per-ha-tee-kan da-rah da-lam oo-reen sah-yah.)*

647. My nose is congested, and I can't smell anything.
Hidung saya tersumbat dan saya tidak bisa mencium apa-apa.
(Hee-doong sah-yah ter-soom-bat dan sah-yah tee-dak bee-sah men-choo-oom ah-pah-ah-pah.)

648. I have a cut that's not healing properly.
Saya memiliki luka yang tidak sembuh dengan baik.
(Sah-yah me-meel-ee-kee loo-kah yahng tee-dak sem-boo de-ngan ba-ik.)

649. My ears have been hurting, and I can't hear well.
Telinga saya sakit dan saya tidak bisa mendengar dengan baik.
(*Tel-eeng-gah sah-yah sah-keet dan sah-yah tee-dak bee-sah men-den-gar de-ngan ba-ik.)*

650. I think I might have a urinary tract infection.
Saya pikir saya mungkin memiliki infeksi saluran kencing.
(Sah-yah pee-keer sah-yah moon-geen me-meel-ee-kee een-fek-see sah-loo-ran ken-ching.)

651. I've had trouble sleeping due to anxiety.
Saya mengalami kesulitan tidur karena kecemasan.
(Sah-yah meng-ah-lah-mee ke-soo-lee-tan tee-door ker-ah-nah ke-che-mah-sahn.)

Requesting Medical Assistance

652. I need to see a doctor urgently.
Saya perlu segera bertemu dengan dokter.
(Sah-yah per-loo seh-ge-rah ber-te-moo de-ngan dok-ter.)

653. Can you call an ambulance, please?
Tolong panggilkan ambulans?
(Toh-long pang-geel-kahn am-boo-lans?)

654. I require immediate medical attention.
Saya membutuhkan perawatan medis segera.
(Sah-yah mem-boo-tooh-kan peh-rah-wah-tan meh-dis seh-geh-rah.)

655. Is there an available appointment today?
Apakah ada janji temu yang tersedia hari ini?
(Ah-pah-kah ah-dah jahn-jee te-moo yahng ter-seh-dee-ah hah-ree ee-nee?)

656. Please help me find a nearby clinic.
Tolong bantu saya menemukan klinik terdekat.
(Toh-long bahn-too sah-yah meh-ne-moo-kahn klee-neek ter-deh-kaht.)

657. I think I'm having a medical emergency.
Saya pikir saya mengalami keadaan darurat medis.
(Sah-yah pee-keer sah-yah meng-ah-lah-mee keh-ah-dah-ahn dah-roo-raht meh-dis.)

658. Can you recommend a specialist?
Bisa merekomendasikan spesialis?
(Bee-sah meh-reh-koh-men-dah-see-kahn speh-see-ah-lees?)

659. I'm in severe pain; can I see a doctor now?
Saya mengalami sakit yang sangat parah; bisakah saya bertemu dokter sekarang?
(Sah-yah meng-ah-lah-mee sah-keet yahng sahng-ahht pah-rah; bee-sah-kah sah-yah ber-teh-moo dok-ter seh-kah-rang?)

660. Is there a 24-hour pharmacy in the area?
Apakah ada apotek yang buka 24 jam di area ini?
(Ah-pah-kah ah-dah ah-po-tek yahng boo-kah yir-mee-dohrt jahm dee ah-re-ah ee-nee?)

661. I need a prescription refill.
Saya perlu mengisi ulang resep saya.
(Sah-yah per-loo men-gee-see oo-lang reh-sep sah-yah.)

662. Can you guide me to the nearest hospital?
Bisakah Anda menunjukkan saya rumah sakit terdekat?
(Bee-sah-kah Ahn-dah meh-noon-jook-kahn sah-yah roo-mah sah-keet ter-deh-kaht?)

663. I've cut myself and need medical assistance.
Saya terluka dan membutuhkan bantuan medis.
(Sah-yah ter-loo-kah dahn mem-boo-tooh-kahn bahn-too-an meh-dis.)

664. My child has a high fever; what should I do?
Anak saya demam tinggi; apa yang harus saya lakukan?
(Ah-nahk sah-yah deh-mahm teen-gee; ah-pah yahng hah-roos sah-yah lah-koo-kahn?)

665. Is there a walk-in clinic nearby?
Apakah ada klinik tanpa janji di dekat sini?
(Ah-pah-kah ah-dah klee-neek tahn-pah jahn-jee dee deh-kaht see-nee?)

666. I need medical advice about my condition.
Saya memerlukan nasihat medis mengenai kondisi saya.
(Sah-yah meh-mer-loo-kahn nah-see-haht meh-dis meng-eh-nai kon-dee-see sah-yah.)

667. My medication has run out; I need a refill.
Obat saya habis; saya perlu isi ulang.
(Oh-baht sah-yah hah-bees; sah-yah per-loo ee-see oo-lang.)

668. Can you direct me to an eye doctor?
Bisakah Anda mengarahkan saya ke dokter mata?
(Bee-sah-kah Ahn-dah meng-ah-rah-kahn sah-yah keh dok-ter mah-tah?)

669. I've been bitten by a dog; I'm concerned.
Saya digigit anjing; saya khawatir.
(Sah-yah dee-gee-geet ahn-jeeng; sah-yah khah-wah-teer.)

670. Is there a dentist available for an emergency?
Apakah ada dokter gigi yang tersedia untuk keadaan darurat?
(Ah-pah-kah ah-dah dok-ter gee-gee yahng ter-seh-dee-ah oon-took keh-ah-dahn dah-roo-raht?)

671. I think I might have food poisoning.
Saya pikir saya mungkin keracunan makanan.
(Sah-yah pee-keer sah-yah mung-keen keh-rah-choo-nahn mah-kah-nahn.)

672. Can you help me find a pediatrician for my child?
Bisakah Anda membantu saya menemukan dokter anak untuk anak saya?
(Bee-sah-kah Ahn-dah mem-bahn-too sah-yah meh-ne-moo-kahn dok-ter ah-nahk oon-took ah-nahk sah-yah?)

Idiomatic Expression: "Tangkap basah." -
Meaning: "Caught red-handed."
(Literal translation: "Caught wet.")

Discussing Medications and Treatments

673. What is this medication for?
Untuk apa obat ini digunakan?
(Oon-took ah-pah oh-baht ee-nee dee-goo-nah-kahn?)

674. How often should I take this pill?
Seberapa sering saya harus minum pil ini?
(Seh-beh-rah seh-reeng sah-yah hah-roos mee-noom peel ee-nee?)

675. Are there any potential side effects?
Apakah ada efek samping yang mungkin?
(Ah-pah-kah ah-dah eh-fek sahm-peeng yahng moong-keen?)

676. Can I take this medicine with food?
Apakah saya bisa minum obat ini dengan makanan?
(Ah-pah-kah sah-yah bee-sah mee-noom oh-baht ee-nee dehng-ahn mah-kah-nahn?)

677. Should I avoid alcohol while on this medication?
Apakah saya harus menghindari alkohol saat minum obat ini?
(Ah-pah-kah sah-yah hah-roos meng-heen-da-ree al-koh-hohl sah-aht mee-noom oh-baht ee-nee?)

678. Is it safe to drive while taking this?
Apakah aman mengemudi saat minum obat ini?
(Ah-pah-kah ah-mahn meng-eh-moo-dee sah-aht mee-noom oh-baht ee-nee?)

679. How long do I need to continue this treatment?
Berapa lama saya perlu melanjutkan pengobatan ini?
(Beh-rah-pah lah-mah sah-yah per-loo meh-lahn-yoot-kahn peng-oh-bah-tahn ee-nee?)

680. Can you explain the dosage instructions?
Bisakah Anda menjelaskan instruksi dosis?
(Bee-sah-kah Ahn-dah men-jeh-lahs-kahn een-strook-see doh-sees?)

681. What should I do if I miss a dose?
Apa yang harus saya lakukan jika saya melewatkan dosis?
(Ah-pah yahng hah-roos sah-yah lah-koo-kahn jee-kah sah-yah meh-leh-waht-kahn doh-sees?)

682. Are there any dietary restrictions?
Apakah ada pembatasan diet?
(Ah-pah-kah ah-dah pem-bah-tah-sahn dee-et?)

Fun Fact: Shadow Puppets, known as Wayang, is a traditional form of puppetry in Indonesia.

683. Can I get a generic version of this medication?
Bisakah saya mendapatkan versi generik dari obat ini?
(Bee-sah-kah sah-yah men-dah-pah-tahn ver-see jeh-neh-reek dah-ree oh-baht ee-nee?)

684. Is there a non-prescription alternative?
Apakah ada alternatif tanpa resep?
(Ah-pah-kah ah-dah al-ter-nah-teef tahn-pah reh-sep?)

685. How should I store this medication?
Bagaimana saya harus menyimpan obat ini?
(Bah-guy-mah-nah sah-yah hah-roos men-yim-pahn oh-baht ee-nee?)

686. Can you show me how to use this inhaler?
Bisakah Anda menunjukkan cara menggunakan inhaler ini?
(Bee-sah-kah Ahn-dah meh-noon-jook-kahn chah-rah meng-goo-nah-kahn een-hah-ler ee-nee?)

687. What's the expiry date of this medicine?
Apa tanggal kedaluwarsa obat ini?
(Ah-pah tahn-gahl keh-dah-loo-wahr-sah oh-baht ee-nee?)

> **Fun Fact:** Indonesian includes loanwords from Dutch, Arabic, Portuguese, and other languages.

688. Do I need to finish the entire course of antibiotics?
Apakah saya perlu menyelesaikan seluruh kursus antibiotik?
(Ah-pah-kah sah-yah per-loo men-yeh-leh-sah-kan seh-loo-rooh kur-soos an-tee-bee-o-teek?)

689. Can I cut these pills in half?
Apakah saya bisa memotong pil ini menjadi dua?
(Ah-pah-kah sah-yah bee-sah meh-moh-tohng peel ee-nee men-jah-dee doo-ah?)

690. Is there an over-the-counter pain reliever you recommend?
Apakah ada obat penghilang rasa sakit tanpa resep yang Anda rekomendasikan?
(Ah-pah-kah ah-dah oh-baht peng-hee-lang rah-sah sah-keet tahn-pah reh-sep yahng Ahn-dah reh-koh-men-dah-see-kahn?)

691. Can I take this medication while pregnant?
Apakah saya bisa mengonsumsi obat ini saat hamil?
(Ah-pah-kah sah-yah bee-sah meng-ohn-soom-see oh-baht ee-nee sah-aht hah-meel?)

692. What should I do if I experience an allergic reaction?
Apa yang harus saya lakukan jika mengalami reaksi alergi?
(Ah-pah yahng hah-roos sah-yah lah-koo-kahn jee-kah meng-ah-lah-mee reh-ak-see ah-lehr-gee?)

> **Fun Fact:** Sanskrit has also significantly influenced Indonesian.

693. Can you provide more information about this treatment plan?
Bisakah Anda memberikan lebih banyak informasi tentang rencana pengobatan ini?
(Bee-sah-kah Ahn-dah mehm-beh-ree-kahn leh-beeh bahn-yahk een-for-mah-see ten-tahng rehn-chah-nah peng-oh-bah-tahn ee-nee?)

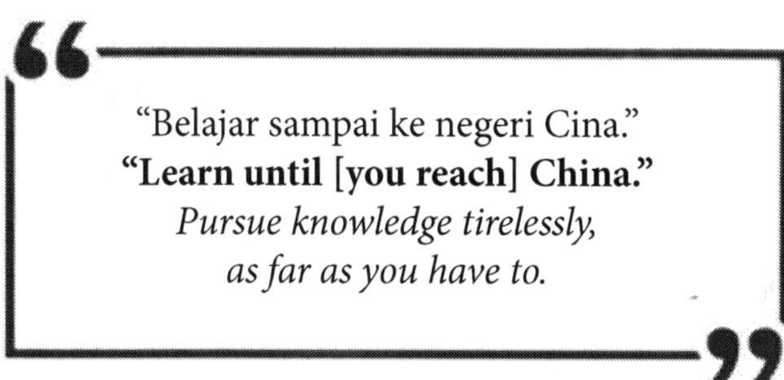

"Belajar sampai ke negeri Cina."
"Learn until [you reach] China."
Pursue knowledge tirelessly, as far as you have to.

Word Search Puzzle: Healthcare

HOSPITAL
RUMAH SAKIT
DOCTOR
DOKTER
MEDICINE
OBAT
PRESCRIPTION
RESEP
APPOINTMENT
JANJI
SURGERY
OPERASI
VACCINE
VAKSIN
PHARMACY
APOTEK
ILLNESS
PENYAKIT
TREATMENT
PERAWATAN
DIAGNOSIS
DIAGNOSA
RECOVERY
PEMULIHAN
SYMPTOM
GEJALA
IMMUNIZATION
IMUNISASI

```
L N F Q Y H I X D E M O M V M
O A A A J A S U R G E R Y A S
D P T X M M D P M Y D M A C S
I I E I R U X T F I I O O C E
A N D R P R D O Q A C T U I N
G P X S A S N O Q Q I P O N L
N O M I K S O T K U N M H E L
O Z A N L V I H P T E Y T S I
S L X W A K G D G I E S N N T
I S J K A C S L P C E R E W W
S I S Y A T O P E A K D M Y I
E I N F I R U L D E I V T R Z
N E K J Y C A M R A H P N K A
P Y N E P W A G G U Z L I S F
R A V X T L X N S F T P O X U
J T Y F A O O D M P D W P V X
N X P J R S P S U K R I P S L
C A E E A D T A T H M N A L S
P G H I S T R E A T M E N T E
C E M I M E N T V T H O W D R
G C R A L U R A B H B G U U X
G Q W A P U N C W A Q K U C N
A Z Z P W C M I T H X K X T T
E A F H P A Y E S H H X A I X
E U F A U J T E P A X D K Z N
G G N K V T C A T M S A X C Y
R D O C T O R N N I S I R P L
S W W N O I T P I R C S E R P
Y R E V O C E R E J A B Q B Q
I M M U N I Z A T I O N P F U
```

Correct Answers:

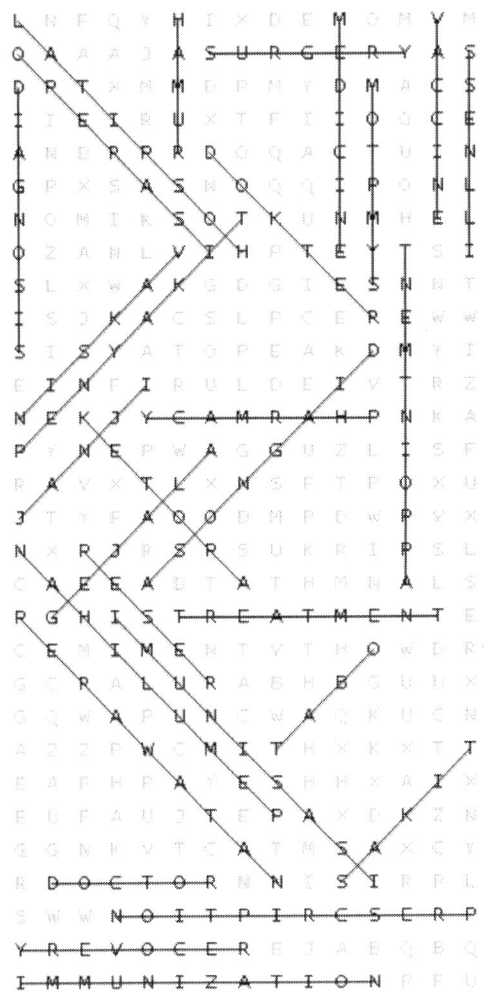

FAMILY & RELATIONSHIPS

- TALKING ABOUT FAMILY MEMBERS & RELATIONSHIPS -
- DISCUSSING PERSONAL LIFE & EXPERIENCES -
- EXPRESSING EMOTIONS & SENTIMENTS -

Family Members and Relationships

694. He's my younger brother.
Dia adalah adik laki-laki saya yang lebih muda.
(Dee-ah ah-dah-lah ah-deek lah-kee-lah-kee sah-yah yahng leh-beeh moo-dah.)

695. She's my cousin from my mother's side.
Dia sepupu saya dari pihak ibu.
(Dee-ah seh-poo-poo sah-yah dah-ree pee-hahk ee-boo.)

696. My grandparents have been married for 50 years.
Kakek dan nenek saya telah menikah selama 50 tahun.
(Kah-kek dan neh-nek sah-yah teh-lah meh-nee-kah seh-lah-mah leem-poo-luh tah-hoon.)

697. We're like sisters from another mister.
Kami seperti saudara perempuan dari ayah yang berbeda.
(Kah-mee seh-per-tee sow-dah-rah peh-rehm-poo-ahn dah-ree ah-yah yahng ber-beh-dah.)

698. He's my husband's best friend.
Dia adalah sahabat terbaik suami saya.
(Dee-ah ah-dah-lah sah-hah-baht tehr-bah-ik soo-ah-mee sah-yah.)

699. She's my niece on my father's side.
Dia adalah keponakan saya dari pihak ayah.
(Dee-ah ah-dah-lah keh-po-nah-kan sah-yah dah-ree pee-hahk ah-yah.)

700. They are my in-laws.
Mereka adalah mertua saya.
(Meh-reh-kah ah-dah-lah mer-too-ah sah-yah.)

701. Our family is quite close-knit.
Keluarga kami sangat erat.
(Keh-loo-ar-gah kah-mee sahng-aht eh-raht.)

702. He's my adopted son.
Dia adalah anak angkat saya.
(Dee-ah ah-dah-lah ah-nahk ahng-kaht sah-yah.)

703. She's my half-sister.
Dia adalah saudara perempuan saya seayah.
(Dee-ah ah-dah-lah sow-dah-rah peh-rehm-poo-ahn sah-yah seh-ah-yah.)

> **Travel Story:** At a serene temple in Lake Toba, a monk described meditation as "Sambil menyelam, minum air," emphasizing the ability to find peace amidst chaos.

704. My parents are divorced.
Orang tua saya bercerai.
(Ohr-ahng too-ah sah-yah ber-cheh-rai.)

705. He's my fiancé.
Dia adalah tunangan saya.
(Dee-ah ah-dah-lah too-nahn-gahn sah-yah.)

706. She's my daughter-in-law.
Dia adalah menantu perempuan saya.
(Dee-ah ah-dah-lah meh-nahn-too peh-rehm-poo-ahn sah-yah.)

> **Idiomatic Expression:** "Potong bebek angsa." - Meaning: "To do something without thinking." (Literal translation: "Slicing the goose and the duck.")

707. We're childhood friends.
Kami adalah teman masa kecil.
(*Kah-mee ah-dah-lah teh-mahn mah-sah keh-cheel.)*

708. My twin brother and I are very close.
Saya dan saudara kembar saya sangat dekat.
(Sah-yah dahn sow-dah-rah kem-bar sah-yah sahng-aht deh-kaht.)

709. He's my godfather.
Dia adalah ayah baptis saya.
(Dee-ah ah-dah-lah ah-yah bap-tis sah-yah.)

710. She's my stepsister.
Dia adalah saudara tiri perempuan saya.
(*Dee-ah ah-dah-lah sow-dah-rah tee-ree peh-rehm-poo-ahn sah-yah.)*

711. My aunt is a world traveler.
Bibi saya adalah seorang pelancong dunia.
(Bee-bee sah-yah ah-dah-lah seh-oh-rang peh-lahn-chong doo-nee-ah.)

712. We're distant relatives.
Kami adalah kerabat jauh.
(Kah-mee ah-dah-lah keh-rah-baht jowh.)

713. He's my brother-in-law.
Dia adalah ipar laki-laki saya.
(Dee-ah ah-dah-lah ee-par lah-kee-lah-kee sah-yah.)

714. She's my ex-girlfriend.
Dia adalah mantan pacar saya.
(Dee-ah ah-dah-lah mahn-tahn pah-char sah-yah.)

Personal Life and Experiences

715. I've traveled to over 20 countries.
Saya telah bepergian ke lebih dari 20 negara.
(Sah-yah teh-lah be-per-gi-ahn ke le-beeh dah-ree doo-ah poo-looh neh-gah-rah.)

716. She's an avid hiker and backpacker.
Dia adalah seorang pendaki dan backpacker yang antusias.
(Dee-ah ah-dah-lah seh-oh-rang pen-dah-kee dan back-packer yang ahn-too-see-as.)

717. I enjoy cooking and trying new recipes.
Saya menikmati memasak dan mencoba resep baru.
(Sah-yah me-nee-keh-mah-tee meh-mah-sak dan men-cho-bah reh-sep bah-roo.)

718. He's a professional photographer.
Dia adalah fotografer profesional.
(Dee-ah ah-dah-lah foh-toh-grah-fer pro-fe-syo-nal.)

719. I'm passionate about environmental conservation.
Saya bersemangat tentang pelestarian lingkungan.
(Sah-yah ber-seh-mahng-aht ten-tang pe-leh-stah-ree-an ling-koong-an.)

720. She's a proud dog owner.
Dia adalah pemilik anjing yang bangga.
(Dee-ah ah-dah-lah peh-mee-leek ahn-jing yang bahng-gah.)

721. I love attending live music concerts.
Saya suka menghadiri konser musik langsung.
(Sah-yah soo-kah meng-hah-dee-ree kon-ser moo-seek lahng-soong.)

722. He's an entrepreneur running his own business.
Dia adalah seorang pengusaha yang menjalankan bisnisnya sendiri.
(Dee-ah ah-dah-lah seh-oh-rang peng-oo-sah-hah yang men-jah-lan-kan beez-nees-nya sen-dee-ree.)

723. I've completed a marathon.
Saya telah menyelesaikan sebuah maraton.
(Sah-yah teh-lah men-ye-les-eye-kan seh-boo-ah mah-rah-ton.)

724. She's a dedicated volunteer at a local shelter.
Dia adalah sukarelawan yang berdedikasi di suaka lokal.
(Dee-ah ah-dah-lah soo-kah-reh-lawan yang ber-deh-dee-kah-see dee soo-ah-kah lo-kahl.)

725. I'm a history buff.
Saya penggemar sejarah.
(Sah-yah peng-ge-mar seh-jah-rah.)

726. He's a bookworm and a literature lover.
Dia adalah kutu buku dan pencinta sastra.
(Dee-ah ah-dah-lah koo-too boo-koo dan pen-cheen-tah sahs-trah.)

727. I've recently taken up painting.
Baru-baru ini saya mulai melukis.
(Bah-roo-bah-roo ee-nee sah-yah moo-lie me-loo-kees.)

728. She's a film enthusiast.
Dia adalah seorang penggemar film.
(Dee-ah ah-dah-lah seh-oh-rang peng-ge-mar feelm.)

729. I enjoy gardening in my free time.
Saya menikmati berkebun di waktu luang saya.
(Sah-yah me-nee-kmah-tee ber-keh-boon dee wah-ktoo loo-ahng sah-yah.)

730. He's an astronomy enthusiast.
Dia adalah penggemar astronomi.
(Dee-ah ah-dah-lah peng-ge-mar as-troh-noh-mee.)

731. I've skydived twice.
Saya telah terjun payung dua kali.
(Sah-yah teh-lah ter-joon pah-yoong doo-ah kah-lee.)

732. She's a fitness trainer.
Dia adalah pelatih kebugaran.
(Dee-ah ah-dah-lah peh-lah-teeh keh-boo-gah-rahn.)

733. I love collecting vintage records.
Saya suka mengumpulkan rekaman vintage.
(Sah-yah soo-kah meng-oom-pool-kahn reh-kah-man vin-tahj.)

734. He's an experienced scuba diver.
Dia adalah penyelam scuba yang berpengalaman.
(Dee-ah ah-dah-lah pen-ye-lahm skoo-bah yang ber-peng-ah-lah-mahn.)

735. I'm a proud parent of three children.
Saya adalah orang tua bangga dari tiga anak.
(Sah-yah ah-dah-lah oh-rang too-ah bahn-gah dah-ree tee-gah ah-nahk.)

Expressing Emotions and Sentiments

736. I feel overjoyed on my birthday.
Saya sangat bahagia di hari ulang tahun saya.
(Sah-yah sahng-aht bah-hah-gee-ah dee hah-ree oo-lahng tah-hoon sah-yah.)

737. She's going through a tough time right now.
Dia sedang mengalami masa sulit saat ini.
(Dee-ah seh-dahng meng-ah-lah-mee mah-sah soo-leet sah-at ee-nee.)

738. I'm thrilled about my upcoming vacation.
Saya sangat bersemangat tentang liburan saya yang akan datang.
(Sah-yah sahng-at ber-seh-mahng-at ten-tang lee-boo-ran sah-yah yang ah-kahn dah-tahng.)

739. He's heartbroken after the breakup.
Dia patah hati setelah putus.
(Dee-ah pah-tah ha-tee seh-teh-lah poo-toos.)

740. I'm absolutely ecstatic about the news.
Saya benar-benar sangat gembira tentang berita tersebut.
(Sah-yah beh-nar-beh-nar sahng-at gem-bee-rah ten-tang beh-ree-tah teh-roo-seh-oot.)

741. She's feeling anxious before the big presentation.
Dia merasa cemas sebelum presentasi besar.
(Dee-ah meh-rah-sah cheh-mahs seh-loo-moohm preh-sen-tah-see beh-sahr.)

742. I'm proud of my team's achievements.
Saya bangga dengan pencapaian tim saya.
(Sah-yah bahng-gah dehng-an pen-chah-pah-ee-an teem sah-yah.)

743. He's devastated by the loss.
Dia sangat terpukul karena kehilangan.
(Dee-ah sahng-at tehr-poo-kool kah-reh-nah keh-hee-lahng-an.)

744. I'm grateful for the support I received.
Saya bersyukur atas dukungan yang saya terima.
(Sah-yah ber-shoo-koor ah-tahs doo-koon-gan yang sah-yah teh-ree-mah.)

745. She's experiencing a mix of emotions.
Dia mengalami campuran emosi.
(Dee-ah meng-ah-lah-mee cham-poo-ran eh-moh-see.)

746. I'm content with where I am in life.
Saya puas dengan posisi saya dalam kehidupan.
(Sah-yah poo-ahs dehng-an poh-see-see sah-yah dah-lahm keh-hee-doo-pahn.)

747. He's overwhelmed by the workload.
Dia merasa kewalahan oleh beban kerja.
(Dee-ah meh-rah-sah keh-wah-lah-han oh-leh beh-ban kehr-jah.)

748. I'm in awe of the natural beauty here.
Saya kagum dengan keindahan alam di sini.
(Sah-yah kah-goom dehng-an kay-een-dah-han ah-lahm dee see-nee.)

Language Learning Tip: Practice with Native Speakers - Conversing with native speakers is invaluable.

749. She's relieved the exams are finally over.
Dia lega karena ujian telah berakhir.
(Dee-ah leh-gah kah-reh-nah oo-jee-an teh-lah ber-ah-keer.)

750. I'm excited about the new job opportunity.
Saya bersemangat tentang kesempatan pekerjaan baru.
(Sah-yah ber-seh-mahng-at ten-tang keh-sehm-pah-tan peh-ker-jah-an bah-roo.)

Travel Story: While snorkeling in Bunaken, a diver mentioned "Bagaikan air di daun keladi," to describe the fleeting beauty of the underwater world.

751. I'm nostalgic about my childhood.
Saya merindukan masa kecil saya.
(Sah-yah meh-rin-doo-kahn mah-sah keh-cheel sah-yah.)

752. She's confused about her future.
Dia bingung tentang masa depannya.
(Dee-ah been-goong ten-tahng mah-sah deh-pahn-nyah.)

753. I'm touched by the kindness of strangers.
Saya tersentuh oleh kebaikan orang asing.
(Sah-yah ter-sen-tooh oh-leh keh-bai-kahn oh-rang ah-seeng.)

754. He's envious of his friend's success.
Dia iri dengan kesuksesan temannya.
(Dee-ah ee-ree deh-ngahn keh-sook-seh-sahn tehm-ahn-nyah.)

755. I'm hopeful for a better tomorrow.
Saya berharap untuk hari esok yang lebih baik.
(Sah-yah ber-hah-rap oon-took hah-ree eh-sohk yahng leh-beeh bah-ik.)

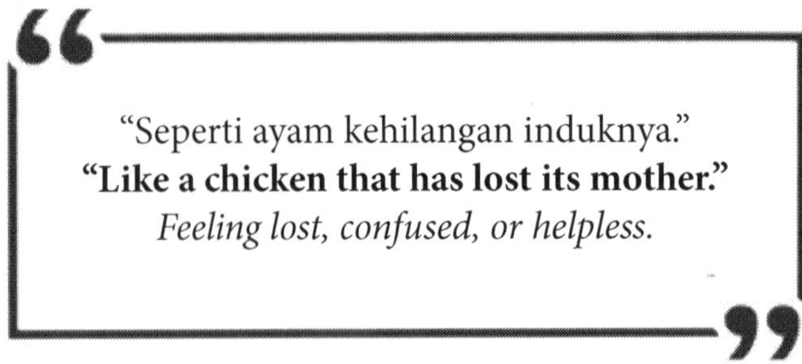

"Seperti ayam kehilangan induknya."
"Like a chicken that has lost its mother."
Feeling lost, confused, or helpless.

Interactive Challenge: Family & Relationships

(Link each English word with their corresponding meaning in Indonesian)

1) Family	Adopsi
2) Parents	Persahabatan
3) Siblings	Keluarga
4) Children	Pernikahan
5) Grandparents	Sepupu
6) Spouse	Keponakan
7) Marriage	Kerabat
8) Love	Orang tua
9) Friendship	Perceraian
10) Relatives	Pasangan
11) In-laws	Saudara kandung
12) Divorce	Mertua
13) Adoption	Kakek dan nenek
14) Cousins	Cinta
15) Niece	Anak-anak

Correct Answers:

1. Family - Keluarga
2. Parents - Orang tua
3. Siblings - Saudara kandung
4. Children - Anak-anak
5. Grandparents - Kakek dan nenek
6. Spouse - Pasangan
7. Marriage - Pernikahan
8. Love - Cinta
9. Friendship - Persahabatan
10. Relatives - Kerabat
11. In-laws - Mertua
12. Divorce - Perceraian
13. Adoption - Adopsi
14. Cousins - Sepupu
15. Niece - Keponakan

TECHNOLOGY & COMMUNICATION

- USING TECHNOLOGY-RELATED PHRASES -
- INTERNET ACCESS AND COMMUNICATION TOOLS -
- TROUBLESHOOTING TECHNICAL ISSUES -

Using Technology

756. I use my smartphone for various tasks.
Saya menggunakan smartphone saya untuk berbagai tugas.
(Sah-yah men-gun-ah-kahn smahr-tfohn sah-yah oon-took ber-bah-gai too-gahs.)

757. The computer is an essential tool in my work.
Komputer adalah alat penting dalam pekerjaan saya.
(*Kom-poo-ter ah-dah-lah ah-laht pen-ting dah-lahm peh-ker-jah-an sah-yah.)*

758. I'm learning how to code and develop software.
Saya sedang belajar cara membuat kode dan mengembangkan perangkat lunak.
(Sah-yah seh-dahng beh-lah-jahr chah-rah mehm-boo-aht ko-deh dan men-gen-bang-kahn peh-rang-kat loo-nahk.)

759. My tablet helps me stay organized.
Tablet saya membantu saya tetap terorganisir.
(Tahb-let sah-yah mem-bahn-too sah-yah teh-tahp ter-or-gah-nee-seer.)

760. I enjoy exploring new apps and software.
Saya menikmati menjelajahi aplikasi dan perangkat lunak baru.
(Sah-yah meh-nee-kmah-tee men-jeh-lah-hi ah-plee-kah-see dan peh-rang-kat loo-nahk bah-roo.)

> **Fun Fact:** The Tourism Hub is a major sector with destinations like Bali and Yogyakarta.

761. Smartwatches are becoming more popular.
Jam tangan pintar semakin populer.
(Jahm tahn-gan pin-tahr seh-mah-keen po-poo-ler.)

762. Virtual reality technology is fascinating.
Teknologi realitas virtual sangat menarik.
(Tek-no-loh-gee reh-ah-lee-tahs vir-too-al sahng-aht meh-nah-reek.)

763. Artificial intelligence is changing industries.
Kecerdasan buatan mengubah industri.
(Keh-chair-dah-san boo-ah-tan men-goo-bah in-doos-tree.)

764. I like to customize my gadgets.
Saya suka mengkustomisasi gadget saya.
(Sah-yah soo-kah meng-kus-toh-mee-sah-see gah-jet sah-yah.)

765. E-books have replaced physical books for me.
E-book telah menggantikan buku fisik bagi saya.
(Eh-book teh-lah meng-gahn-tee-kahn boo-koo fee-seek bah-ghee sah-yah.)

766. Social media platforms connect people worldwide.
Platform media sosial menghubungkan orang di seluruh dunia.
(Plat-form meh-dee-ah soh-syah-al meng-hoo-boong-kahn oh-rang dee seh-loo-rooh doo-nee-ah.)

767. I'm a fan of wearable technology.
Saya penggemar teknologi yang dapat dipakai.
(Sah-yah peng-geh-mar tek-no-loh-gee yahng dah-pat dee-pah-kai.)

768. The latest gadgets always catch my eye.
Gadget terbaru selalu menarik perhatian saya.
(Gah-jet ter-bah-roo seh-lah-loo meh-nah-reek per-hah-tee-an sah-yah.)

769. My digital camera captures high-quality photos.
Kamera digital saya mengambil foto berkualitas tinggi.
(Kah-me-rah di-jee-tal sah-yah meng-ahm-beel fo-to ber-koo-ah-lee-tahs teen-gee.)

770. Home automation simplifies daily tasks.
Otomatisasi rumah mempermudah tugas harian.
(O-toh-mah-tee-sah-see roo-mah mem-per-moo-dah too-gas ha-ree-an.)

771. I'm into 3D printing as a hobby.
Saya menyukai pencetakan 3D sebagai hobi.
(Sah-yah men-yoo-ka-ee pen-che-tah-kahn tee-ga deh seh-bah-guy hoh-bee.)

772. Streaming services have revolutionized entertainment.
Layanan streaming telah merevolusi hiburan.
(Lah-yah-nan stre-ming teh-lah me-re-vo-loo-see hee-boo-ran.)

773. The Internet of Things (IoT) is expanding.
Internet of Things (IoT) sedang berkembang.
(Een-ter-net ov teengs se-dahng ber-kem-bahng.)

774. I'm into gaming, both console and PC.
Saya tertarik pada permainan, baik konsol dan PC.
(Sah-yah ter-tah-reek pah-dah per-mai-nan, baik kon-sol dan pee-ce.)

775. Wireless headphones make life more convenient.
Headphone nirkabel membuat hidup lebih praktis.
(Head-phone neer-kah-bel mem-boo-aht hee-doop le-beeh prak-tis.)

776. Cloud storage is essential for my work.
Penyimpanan awan sangat penting untuk pekerjaan saya.
(Pen-yeem-pah-nan ah-wan sahng-aht pen-ting oon-took peh-ker-jah-an sah-yah.)

> **Travel Story:** During a trek to Mount Bromo, a fellow hiker described the sunrise as "Memukau bagai emas," meaning "Mesmerizing like gold," to capture the breathtaking view.

Internet Access and Communication Tools

777. I rely on high-speed internet for work.
Saya bergantung pada internet kecepatan tinggi untuk pekerjaan.
(Sah-yah ber-gan-toong pah-dah een-ter-net ke-che-pah-tan teen-gee oon-took peh-ker-jah-an.)

778. Video conferencing is crucial for remote meetings.
Konferensi video sangat penting untuk pertemuan jarak jauh.
(Kon-fe-ren-see vi-de-o sahng-aht pen-ting oon-took per-te-moo-an jar-ak jawh.)

779. Social media helps me stay connected with friends.
Media sosial membantu saya tetap terhubung dengan teman.
(Me-dia soh-syal mem-ban-too sah-yah te-tap ter-hoo-boong deh-ngahn teh-man.)

780. Email is my primary mode of communication.
Email adalah mode komunikasi utama saya.
(Ee-mayl ah-dah-lah moh-deh ko-moo-nee-kah-see oo-tah-mah sah-yah.)

781. I use messaging apps to chat with family.
Saya menggunakan aplikasi pesan untuk mengobrol dengan keluarga.
(Sah-yah meng-goon-ah-kan ah-plee-kah-see peh-san oon-took meng-oh-brol deh-ngan keh-loo-ahr-gah.)

782. Voice and video calls keep me in touch with loved ones.
Panggilan suara dan video membuat saya tetap berhubungan dengan orang-orang terkasih.
(Pang-gee-lan soo-ah-rah dan vi-deo meh-mboo-at sah-yah te-tap ber-hoob-oon-gan deh-ngan oh-rang oh-rang ter-ka-seeh.)

783. Online forums are a great source of information.
Forum online merupakan sumber informasi yang bagus.
(Fo-rum on-line mer-oop-ah-kan soom-ber in-for-mah-see yahng bah-goos.)

784. I trust encrypted messaging services for privacy.
Saya percaya pada layanan pesan terenkripsi untuk privasi.
(Sah-yah per-chah-yah pah-dah lah-yah-nan peh-san ter-en-krip-see oon-took pree-vah-see.)

785. Webinars are a valuable resource for learning.
Webinar merupakan sumber belajar yang berharga.
(Web-ee-nar mer-oop-ah-kan soom-ber bel-ah-jar yahng ber-har-gah.)

Idiomatic Expression: "Tertipu mulut manis." -
Meaning: "Deceived by sweet words."
(Literal translation: "Fooled by a sweet mouth.")

786. VPNs enhance online security and privacy.
VPN meningkatkan keamanan dan privasi online.
(Vee-Pee-En me-ning-kat-kan keh-ah-mah-nan dan pree-vah-see on-line.)

787. Cloud-based collaboration tools are essential for teamwork.
Alat kolaborasi berbasis cloud sangat penting untuk kerja tim.
(Ah-lat ko-lah-boh-rah-see ber-bah-sees cloud sahng-at pen-ting oon-took ker-jah teem.)

788. I prefer using a wireless router at home.
Saya lebih suka menggunakan router nirkabel di rumah.
(Sah-yah le-beeh soo-kah meng-goon-ah-kan roo-ter neer-kah-bel dee roo-mah.)

789. Online banking simplifies financial transactions.
Perbankan online mempermudah transaksi keuangan.
(Per-bang-kan on-line mem-per-moo-dah trahn-sahk-see keh-oo-ang-an.)

Fun Fact: Indonesian once used traditional scripts like Kawi and Rencong.

790. VoIP services are cost-effective for international calls.
Layanan VoIP efektif biaya untuk panggilan internasional.
(Lah-yah-nan Vo-ee-Pee eh-fek-teef bee-ah-yah oon-took pang-gee-lan in-ter-nah-see-oh-nal.)

791. I enjoy online shopping for convenience.
Saya menikmati belanja online karena kemudahannya.
(Sah-yah meh-nee-kmah-tee bel-ahn-jah on-line keh-reh-nah keh-moo-dah-ahn-yah.)

792. Social networking sites connect people globally.
Situs jejaring sosial menghubungkan orang-orang secara global.
(See-toos jeh-jah-ring soh-see-ahl meng-hoo-boong-kan oh-rang oh-rang se-kah-rah gloh-bal.)

793. E-commerce platforms offer a wide variety of products.
Platform e-commerce menawarkan berbagai macam produk.
(Plat-form eh-kom-ers me-na-wark-an ber-ba-gai ma-cham pro-duk.)

> **Idiomatic Expression:** "Lautan api." - Meaning: "A very difficult situation." (Literal translation: "Sea of fire.")

794. Mobile banking apps make managing finances easy.
Aplikasi perbankan mobile memudahkan pengelolaan keuangan.
(Ap-lee-kah-see per-bang-kan mo-bil me-mu-dah-kan peng-e-lo-lah-an ke-u-ang-an.)

795. I'm active on professional networking sites.
Saya aktif di situs jejaring profesional.
(Sah-yah ak-teef dee see-toos je-jar-ing pro-fe-syo-nal.)

796. Virtual private networks protect my online identity.
Jaringan privat virtual melindungi identitas online saya.
(Jar-ing-an pri-vat vir-tu-al me-lin-doon-gee i-den-ti-tas on-line sah-yah.)

797. Instant messaging apps are great for quick chats.
Aplikasi pesan instan sangat bagus untuk obrolan cepat.
(Ap-lee-kah-see pe-san in-stan sang-at ba-gus oon-took ob-ro-lan che-pat.)

> **Cultural Insight:** Tea drinking is a prevalent culture, with regions like West Java known for their tea plantations.

Troubleshooting Technical Issues

798. My computer is running slow; I need to fix it.
Komputer saya berjalan lambat; saya perlu memperbaikinya.
(Kom-pu-ter sah-yah ber-ja-lan lam-bat; sah-yah per-loo mem-per-ba-ik-i-nyah.)

799. I'm experiencing network connectivity problems.
Saya mengalami masalah koneksi jaringan.
(Sah-yah meng-a-la-mi ma-sa-lah ko-nek-see jar-ing-an.)

800. The printer isn't responding to my print commands.
Printer tidak merespon perintah cetak saya.
(Prin-ter tee-dak me-re-spon pe-rin-tah che-tak sah-yah.)

> **Fun Fact:** Indonesia is third in the world for biodiversity, after Brazil and Colombia.

801. My smartphone keeps freezing; it's frustrating.
Ponsel pintar saya terus menerus membeku; ini membuat frustrasi.
(Pon-sel pin-tar sah-yah te-rus me-ne-rus mem-be-ku; ee-nee me-mboo-at frus-tra-see.)

802. The Wi-Fi signal in my house is weak.
Sinyal Wi-Fi di rumah saya lemah.
(Sin-yal Vee-Fee dee roo-mah sah-yah le-mah.)

803. I can't access certain websites; it's a concern.
Saya tidak bisa mengakses beberapa situs web; ini menjadi kekhawatiran.
(Sah-yah tee-dak bee-sah meng-ak-ses be-ber-a-pah see-toos web; ee-nee men-jah-dee ke-khaw-at-ee-ran.)

804. My laptop battery drains quickly; I need a solution.
Baterai laptop saya cepat habis; saya membutuhkan solusi.
(Ba-te-rai la-top sah-yah che-pat ha-bis; sah-yah mem-bu-tuh-kan so-lu-si.)

805. There's a software update available for my device.
Ada pembaruan perangkat lunak tersedia untuk perangkat saya.
(Ah-da pem-ba-ru-an pe-rang-kat lu-nak ter-se-di-ah oon-took pe-rang-kat sah-yah.)

806. My email account got locked; I need to recover it.
Akun email saya terkunci; saya perlu memulihkannya.
(Ah-koon ee-mel sah-yah ter-koon-chee; sah-yah per-loo me-mu-lih-kan-nyah.)

Fun Fact: Indonesia is the world's largest producer of palm oil.

807. The screen on my tablet is cracked; I'm upset.
Layar tablet saya retak; saya kesal.
(Lah-yar ta-blet sah-yah re-tak; sah-yah ke-sal.)

808. My webcam isn't working during video calls.
Webcam saya tidak berfungsi saat panggilan video.
(Web-kam sah-yah tee-dak ber-fung-si saat pang-gee-lan vi-de-o.)

809. My phone's storage is almost full; I need to clear it.
Penyimpanan ponsel saya hampir penuh; saya perlu membersihkannya.
(Pen-yim-pa-nan pon-sel sah-yah ham-pir pe-nuh; sah-yah per-loo mem-ber-sih-kan-nyah.)

810. I accidentally deleted important files; I need help.
Saya secara tidak sengaja menghapus file penting; saya membutuhkan bantuan.
(Sah-yah se-ca-ra tee-dak seng-a-ja meng-ha-pus file pen-ting; sah-yah mem-bu-tuh-kan ban-tu-an.)

> **Fun Fact:** The Jatiluwih rice terraces in Bali are a UNESCO World Heritage Site.

811. My smart home devices are not responding.
Perangkat rumah pintar saya tidak merespons.
(Pe-rang-kat ru-mah pin-tar sah-yah tee-dak me-re-spons.)

812. The GPS on my navigation app is inaccurate.
GPS pada aplikasi navigasi saya tidak akurat.
(Je-Pe-Es pa-da ap-li-ka-si na-vi-ga-si sah-yah tee-dak a-koo-rat.)

813. My antivirus software detected a threat; I'm worried.
Perangkat lunak antivirus saya mendeteksi ancaman; saya khawatir.
(Pe-rang-kat lu-nak an-tee-vi-rus sah-yah men-de-tek-si an-ca-man; sah-yah kha-wa-teer.)

814. The touchscreen on my device is unresponsive.
Layar sentuh pada perangkat saya tidak merespons.
(Lah-yar sen-tuh pa-da pe-rang-kat sah-yah tee-dak me-re-spons.)

815. My gaming console is displaying error messages.
Konsol game saya menampilkan pesan kesalahan.
(Kon-sol ga-me sah-yah me-nam-pil-kan pe-san ke-sa-lah-an.)

816. I'm locked out of my social media account.
Saya terkunci dari akun media sosial saya.
(Sah-yah ter-koon-chee dar-ree ah-koon meh-dee-ah so-syal sah-yah.)

817. The sound on my computer is distorted.
Suara di komputer saya terdistorsi.
(Soo-ah-rah dee kom-poo-ter sah-yah ter-dis-tor-see.)

818. My email attachments won't open; it's frustrating.
Lampiran email saya tidak bisa dibuka; ini sangat mengesalkan.
(Lam-peer-an e-mail sah-yah tee-dak bee-sah dee-boo-kah; ee-nee sang-at meng-eh-sal-kan.)

"Buku adalah jendela dunia."
"Books are the windows to the world."
Reading broadens one's horizons and knowledge.

Cross Word Puzzle: Technology & Communication

(Provide the English translation for the following Indonesian words)

Down

1. - KOMPUTER
2. - PENGISI DAYA
4. - PAPAN KETIK
6. - PINTU MASUK
8. - KRIPTOLOGI
10. - INTERNET
13. - DATA

Across

3. - BATERAI
5. - PERAMBAN
7. - JARINGAN
9. - PENCETAK
11. - APLIKASI
12. - AWAN
14. - LAYAR
15. - ROUTER
16. - KAMERA WEB

Correct Answers:

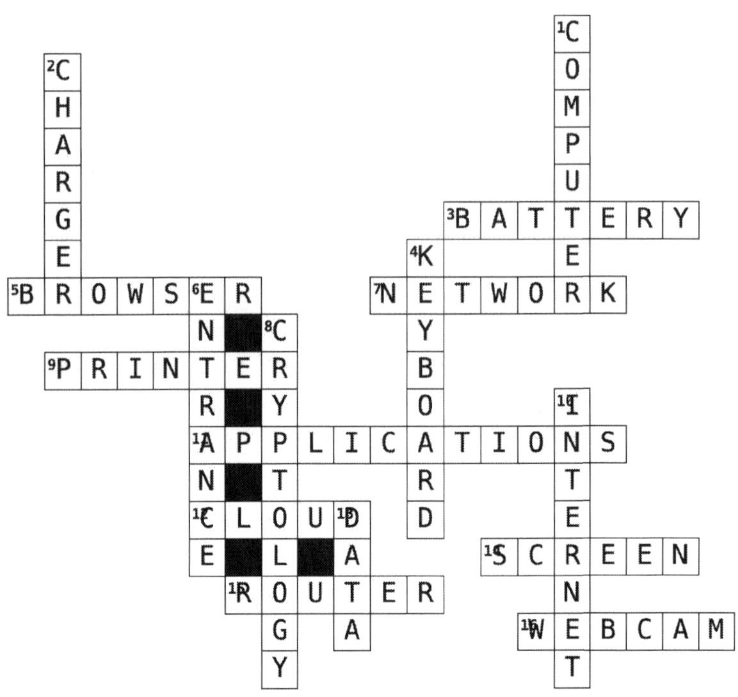

SPORTS & RECREATION

- DISCUSSING SPORTS, GAMES, & OUTDOOR ACTIVITIES -
- PARTICIPATING IN RECREATIONAL ACTIVITIES -
- EXPRESSING ENTHUSUASM OR FRUSTRATION -

Sports, Games, & Outdoor Activities

819. I love playing soccer with my friends.
Saya suka bermain sepak bola bersama teman-teman saya.
(Sah-yah soo-kah ber-mine sep-ak bo-lah ber-sah-mah te-man-te-man sah-yah.)

820. Basketball is a fast-paced and exciting sport.
Bola basket adalah olahraga yang cepat dan menyenangkan.
(Bo-lah bas-ket ah-dalah o-lah-ra-gah yang che-pat dan men-ye-nang-kan.)

821. Let's go for a hike in the mountains this weekend.
Ayo mendaki gunung akhir pekan ini.
(Ah-yo men-da-kee goo-nung ak-hir pe-kan ee-nee.)

822. Playing chess helps improve my strategic thinking.
Bermain catur membantu meningkatkan berpikir strategis saya.
(Ber-mine cha-toor mem-ban-too me-ning-kat-kan ber-peek-ir stra-te-gis sah-yah.)

823. I'm a fan of tennis; it requires a lot of skill.
Saya penggemar tenis; ini memerlukan banyak keterampilan.
(Sah-yah peng-ge-mar te-nis; ee-nee me-me-ru-lu-kan ban-yak ke-ter-am-pil-an.)

824. Are you up for a game of volleyball at the beach?
Apakah kamu ingin bermain bola voli di pantai?
(Ah-pa-kah ka-moo een-gin ber-mine bo-lah vo-lee dee pan-tai?)

825. Let's organize a game of ultimate frisbee.
Mari kita atur permainan frisbee ultimate.
(Ma-ree kee-tah ah-toor per-mai-nan fris-bee ul-ti-mate.)

826. Baseball games are a great way to spend the afternoon.
Pertandingan bisbol adalah cara yang bagus untuk menghabiskan sore hari.
(Per-tan-ding-an bis-bol ah-dalah cha-rah yang bah-gus un-took meng-ha-bis-kan sore hah-ree.)

827. Camping in the wilderness is so peaceful.
Berkemah di alam liar sangat menenangkan.
(Ber-ke-mah dee ah-lam lee-ar sang-at me-nen-ang-kan.)

828. I enjoy swimming in the local pool.
Saya menikmati berenang di kolam renang lokal.
(Sah-yah me-nee-kmah-tee ber-eh-nang dee ko-lam re-nang lo-kal.)

829. I'm learning to play the guitar in my free time.
Saya sedang belajar bermain gitar di waktu luang saya.
(Sah-yah se-dang be-lah-jar ber-mine gee-tar dee wah-ktoo loo-ang sah-yah.)

830. Skiing in the winter is an exhilarating experience.
Bermain ski di musim dingin adalah pengalaman yang mendebarkan.
(Ber-mine skee dee moo-seem deen-geen ah-dalah peng-ah-lah-man yang men-de-bar-kan.)

831. Going fishing by the lake is so relaxing.
Memancing di danau sangat menenangkan.
(Me-man-ching dee da-now sang-at me-nen-ang-kan.)

832. We should have a board game night with friends.
Kita sebaiknya mengadakan malam permainan papan bersama teman-teman.
(Kee-tah se-bai-knee-ah meng-ah-dah-kan mah-lam per-mai-nan pah-pan ber-sah-mah te-man-te-man.)

833. Martial arts training keeps me fit and disciplined.
Latihan seni bela diri membuat saya tetap bugar dan disiplin.
(Lah-tee-han se-nee be-lah dee-ree me-mboo-at sah-yah teh-tap boo-gar dan dee-si-pleen.)

834. I'm a member of a local running club.
Saya anggota klub lari lokal.
(Sah-yah ahng-go-tah kloob lah-ree loh-kal.)

835. Playing golf is a great way to unwind.
Bermain golf adalah cara yang bagus untuk bersantai.
(Ber-mine golf ah-dalah chah-rah yahng bah-goos un-took ber-san-tie.)

> **Idiomatic Expression:** "Makan hati." -
> Meaning: "To feel deeply upset."
> (Literal translation: "Eating one's heart.")

836. Yoga classes help me stay flexible and calm.
Kelas yoga membantu saya tetap lentur dan tenang.
(Ke-las yo-gah mem-bahn-too sah-yah teh-tap len-toor dan teh-nahng.)

837. I can't wait to go snowboarding this season.
Saya tidak sabar untuk snowboarding musim ini.
(Sah-yah tee-dahk sah-bar un-took snoh-board-ing moo-seem ee-nee.)

838. Going kayaking down the river is an adventure.
Berperahu kano di sungai adalah petualangan.
(Ber-peh-ra-hoo kah-no dee soong-gie ah-dalah pe-too-al-ang-an.)

839. Let's organize a picnic in the park.
Mari kita mengadakan piknik di taman.
(Mah-ree kee-tah meng-ah-dah-kahn pik-neek dee tah-man.)

Participating in Recreational Activities

840. I enjoy painting landscapes as a hobby.
Saya menikmati melukis pemandangan sebagai hobi.
(Sah-yah me-nee-kmah-tee meh-loo-kees peh-man-dang-an seh-bah-gie ho-bee.)

841. Gardening is a therapeutic way to spend my weekends.
Berkebun adalah cara terapeutik untuk menghabiskan akhir pekan saya.
(Ber-ke-boon ah-dalah chah-rah teh-ra-oo-tik un-took meng-hah-bees-kan ak-heer pe-kahn sah-yah.)

842. Playing the piano is my favorite pastime.
Bermain piano adalah cara favorit saya menghabiskan waktu.
(Ber-mine pee-ah-no ah-dalah chah-rah fah-vo-reet sah-yah meng-hah-bees-kan wah-ktoo.)

843. Reading books helps me escape into different worlds.
Membaca buku membantu saya melarikan diri ke dunia lain.
(Mem-bah-chah boo-koo mem-bahn-too sah-yah meh-lah-ree-kahn dee-ree keh doo-nee-ah lie-yn.)

844. I'm a regular at the local dance classes.
Saya rutin mengikuti kelas tari lokal.
(Sah-yah roo-teen meng-ee-koo-tee ke-las tah-ree loh-kal.)

845. Woodworking is a skill I've been honing.
Pengerjaan kayu adalah keterampilan yang saya asah.
(Peng-er-jah-an kah-yoo ah-dalah ke-teh-ram-pil-an yahng sah-yah ah-sah.)

846. I find solace in birdwatching at the nature reserve.
Saya menemukan ketenangan dalam mengamati burung di cagar alam.
(Sah-yah meh-nem-oo-kan ke-te-nang-an da-lam meng-a-ma-tee boor-ung dee cha-gar ah-lam.)

847. Meditation and mindfulness keep me centered.
Meditasi dan kesadaran penuh membuat saya tetap fokus.
(Meh-di-ta-see dan ke-sa-dar-an pe-nooh meh-mboo-at sah-yah teh-tap fo-kus.)

848. I've taken up photography to capture moments.
Saya mulai fotografi untuk menangkap momen.
(Sah-yah moo-lie fo-to-gra-fee un-took me-nang-kap mo-men.)

849. Going to the gym is part of my daily routine.
Pergi ke gym adalah bagian dari rutinitas harian saya.
(Per-gee ke gym ah-dalah bah-gian da-ree roo-tee-nee-tas ha-ree-an sah-yah.)

850. Cooking new recipes is a creative outlet for me.
Memasak resep baru adalah cara kreatif untuk saya.
(Meh-ma-sak re-sep bah-roo ah-dalah cha-rah kreh-a-teef un-took sah-yah.)

851. Building model airplanes is a fascinating hobby.
Membuat model pesawat adalah hobi yang menarik.
(Mem-boo-at mo-del pe-sa-wat ah-dalah ho-bee yahng meh-nah-reek.)

852. I love attending art exhibitions and galleries.
Saya suka menghadiri pameran seni dan galeri.
(Sah-yah soo-kah meng-ha-dee-ree pa-meh-ran se-nee dan ga-le-ree.)

853. Collecting rare stamps has been a lifelong passion.
Mengumpulkan perangko langka telah menjadi gairah sepanjang hidup.
(*Meng-oom-pool-kan pe-rang-ko lang-kah teh-lah men-jah-dee gai-rah se-pan-jang hee-doop.)*

854. I'm part of a community theater group.
Saya bagian dari grup teater komunitas.
(Sah-yah bah-gian da-ree groop teh-ah-ter ko-moo-nee-tas.)

855. Birdwatching helps me connect with nature.
Mengamati burung membantu saya terhubung dengan alam.
(Meng-a-ma-tee boor-ung mem-ban-too sah-yah ter-hoob-oong de-ngan ah-lam.)

856. I'm an avid cyclist and explore new trails.
Saya seorang pesepeda yang antusias dan menjelajahi jalur baru.
(*Sah-yah se-o-rang pe-se-pe-dah yahng an-too-see-as dan men-je-la-jahi ja-loor bah-roo.)*

857. Pottery classes allow me to express myself.
Kelas gerabah memungkinkan saya untuk mengekspresikan diri.
(Ke-las ge-ra-bah me-mung-kin-kan sah-yah un-took men-gek-spres-ee-kan dee-ree.)

858. Playing board games with family is a tradition.
Bermain permainan papan bersama keluarga adalah tradisi.
(Ber-mine per-mai-nan pa-pan ber-sa-mah ke-loo-ar-gah ah-da lah tra-dee-see.)

859. I'm practicing mindfulness through meditation.
Saya mempraktikkan kesadaran penuh melalui meditasi.
(Sah-yah mem-prak-tek-kan ke-sa-dar-an pe-nooh meh-la-loo-ee meh-di-ta-see.)

860. I enjoy long walks in the park with my dog.
Saya menikmati berjalan-jalan panjang di taman bersama anjing saya.
(Sah-yah meh-nee-kmah-tee ber-jah-lan-jah-lan pah-njang dee tah-mahn ber-sah-mah ahn-jing sah-yah.)

> **Travel Story:** In a tranquil village in West Sumatra, a local described their peaceful life as "Seperti air mengalir," or "Like water flowing," symbolizing a life of ease and simplicity.

Expressing Enthusiasm or Frustration

861. I'm thrilled we won the championship!
Saya sangat senang kita memenangkan kejuaraan!
(Sah-yah sahng-ah sen-ahng kee-tah meh-meh-nang-kahn keh-joo-ah-rahn!)

862. Scoring that goal felt amazing.
Mencetak gol itu terasa luar biasa.
(Men-cheh-tahk gohl ee-too teh-rah-sah loo-ar bee-ah-sah.)

863. It's so frustrating when we lose a game.
Sangat mengecewakan saat kita kalah dalam permainan.
(Sahng-ahat men-geh-che-wah-kahn sah-aht kee-tah kah-lah dahl-ahm per-mah-ee-nahn.)

864. I can't wait to play again next week.
Saya tidak sabar untuk bermain lagi minggu depan.
(Sah-yah tee-dahk sah-bar oon-took ber-mah-een lah-gee meeng-goo deh-pahn.)

> **Fun Fact:** Indonesian Cuisine is known for its diverse and rich flavors, including dishes like Nasi Goreng.

865. Our team's performance was outstanding.
Penampilan tim kami luar biasa.
(Pen-ahm-pee-lahn teem kah-mee loo-ar bee-ah-sah.)

866. We need to practice more; we keep losing.
Kita perlu latihan lebih banyak; kita terus kalah.
(Kee-tah per-loo lah-tee-hahn leh-bee bah-nyahk; kee-tah teh-roos kah-lah.)

867. I'm over the moon about our victory!
Saya sangat bahagia dengan kemenangan kita!
(Sah-yah sahng-ah bah-hah-ghee-ah deh-ngahn keh-meh-nang-ahn kee-tah!)

> **Language Learning Tip:** Cook Indonesian Recipes - Learn the names of ingredients and cooking verbs.

868. I'm an avid cyclist and explore new trails.
Saya seorang pesepeda yang antusias dan menjelajahi jalur baru.
(Sah-yah seh-oh-rahng peh-seh-peh-dah yahng ahn-too-see-ahs dahn men-jeh-lah-jah-hee jah-loor bah-roo.)

869. The referee's decision was unfair.
Keputusan wasit itu tidak adil.
(Keh-poo-too-sahn wah-seet ee-too tee-dahk ah-deel.)

870. We've been on a winning streak lately.
Akhir-akhir ini kita sedang dalam rentetan kemenangan.
(Ahk-heer ahk-heer ee-nee kee-tah seh-dahng dahl-ahm rehn-teh-tahn keh-meh-nang-ahn.)

871. I'm disappointed in our team's performance.
Saya kecewa dengan penampilan tim kami.
(Sah-yah keh-che-wah deh-ngahn pen-ahm-pee-lahn teem kah-mee.)

872. The adrenaline rush during the race was incredible.
Ledakan adrenalin selama perlombaan itu luar biasa.
(Leh-dah-kahn ad-reh-na-leen se-lah-mah per-lom-bah-an ee-too loo-ar bee-ah-sah.)

873. We need to step up our game to compete.
Kami perlu meningkatkan permainan kami untuk bersaing.
(Kah-mee per-loo meh-ning-kat-kahn per-mah-ee-nahn kah-mee oon-took ber-sah-ing.)

874. Winning the tournament was a dream come true.
Memenangkan turnamen itu seperti mimpi menjadi kenyataan.
(Meh-men-ang-kahn tur-nah-men ee-too se-per-tee meem-pee mehn-jah-dee keh-nya-tah-an.)

875. I was so close to scoring a goal.
Saya hampir mencetak gol.
(Sah-yah hahm-peer men-cheh-tahk gohl.)

876. We should celebrate our recent win.
Kita harus merayakan kemenangan terbaru kita.
(Kee-tah hah-roos meh-rah-yah-kahn keh-me-nang-ahn ter-bah-roo kee-tah.)

877. Losing by a narrow margin is frustrating.
Kalah dengan selisih tipis itu membuat frustrasi.
(Kah-lah deh-ngahn se-lee-sih tee-pees ee-too mehm-boo-aht froo-strah-see.)

878. Let's train harder to improve our skills.
Mari kita berlatih lebih keras untuk meningkatkan kemampuan kita.
(Mah-ree kee-tah ber-lah-teeh leh-beeh keh-rahs oon-took meh-ning-kat-kahn keh-mam-poo-an kee-tah.)

879. The match was intense from start to finish.
Pertandingan itu intens dari awal hingga akhir.
(Per-tahn-dee-ngahn ee-too in-tens dah-ree ah-wahl heeng-gah ahk-heer.)

880. I'm proud of our team's sportsmanship.
Saya bangga dengan sportivitas tim kami.
(Sah-yah bahng-gah deh-ngahn spor-tee-vee-tas teem kah-mee.)

881. We've faced tough competition this season.
Kami menghadapi persaingan yang keras musim ini.
(Kah-mee mehng-hah-dah-pee per-sigh-ing yahng keh-rahs moo-seem ee-nee.)

882. I'm determined to give it my all in the next game.
Saya bertekad untuk memberikan segalanya di pertandingan berikutnya.
(Sah-yah ber-teh-kahd oon-took mehm-ber-ee-kahn seh-gah-lah-nya dee per-tahn-dee-ngahn ber-ee-koot-nyah.)

"Air tenang menghanyutkan."
"Still waters run deep."
People who seem quiet or passive may have hidden depths of knowledge or experience.

Mini Lesson:
Basic Grammar Principles in Indonesian #3

Introduction:

Welcome to the third installment of our Indonesian grammar series. Building upon the foundational elements and intermediate structures we've covered previously, this lesson will dive into some of the more intricate aspects of Indonesian grammar. These advanced concepts are key to a deeper understanding of the language and will enhance your ability to communicate effectively in Indonesian.

1. Reduplication:

Reduplication in Indonesian is used for a variety of purposes, including forming plurals, intensifying meaning, or indicating a continuous or habitual action.

- *Buku (book) -> Buku-buku (books)*
- *Jalan (walk) -> Jalan-jalan (to take a walk, leisurely)*

2. Affixes:

Indonesian employs a range of prefixes, suffixes, and infixes to alter the meaning of base words, often changing the class of the word (like from a noun to a verb).

- *Ter- (prefix for passive or superlative): Terkenal (famous)*
- *-kan (suffix for causative verbs): Makan (eat) -> Makanan (food)*

3. Particle Usage:

Particles like "lah", "kah", and "pun" are commonly used in Indonesian to express emphasis, form questions, or indicate inclusivity or exclusivity.

- *Sudahlah (enough already)*
- *Maukah kamu? (Would you want to?)*

4. Imperatives:

Imperative forms in Indonesian are used to give commands or make requests, and they often omit the subject.

- *Buka pintu! (Open the door!)*
- *Tolong duduk. (Please sit.)*

5. Interrogative Words:

Indonesian interrogative words are used to form questions, and their placement can vary in the sentence.

- *Siapa (who), Apa (what), Di mana (where), Kapan (when), Mengapa (why)*

6. Conjunctions:

Conjunctions are used to connect words, phrases, or clauses. Common conjunctions include "dan" (and), "atau" (or), "tetapi" (but), and "karena" (because).

- *Saya suka kopi dan teh. (I like coffee and tea.)*

7. Numerals and Counting:

Indonesian uses a decimal numeral system, and counting involves combining these basic numbers.

- *Satu (one), Dua (two), Tiga (three)*

Conclusion:

Mastering these advanced elements of Indonesian grammar will enable you to form more complex sentences and deepen your understanding of the language's nuances. Regular practice, engaging with native speakers, and exposure to Indonesian media will help solidify these concepts. Selamat belajar! (Happy learning!)

TRANSPORT & DIRECTIONS

- ASKING FOR AND GIVING DIRECTIONS -
- USING TRANSPORTATION-RELATED PHRASES -

Asking for and Giving Directions

883. Can you tell me how to get to the nearest subway station?
Bisakah Anda memberitahu saya cara menuju stasiun kereta bawah tanah terdekat?
(Bee-sah-kah Ahn-dah mehm-beh-ree-tah-hoo sah-yah kah-rah meh-noo-joo stah-see-oon keh-reh-tah bah-wah tah-nah ter-deh-kaht?)

884. Excuse me, where's the bus stop for Route 25?
Permisi, di mana halte bus untuk Rute 25?
(Per-mee-see, dee mah-nah hahl-teh boos oon-took Roo-teh dwah-poo-loh leem-ah?)

885. Could you give me directions to the city center?
Bisa Anda beri saya petunjuk ke pusat kota?
(Bee-sah Ahn-dah beh-ree sah-yah peh-toon-joohk keh poo-saht koh-tah?)

886. I'm looking for a good place to eat around here. Any recommendations?
Saya mencari tempat makan yang bagus di sekitar sini. Ada rekomendasi?
(Sah-yah men-char-ee tem-paht mah-kahn yahng bah-goos dee seh-kee-tahr see-nee. Ah-dah reh-koh-men-dah-see?)

887. Which way is the nearest pharmacy?
Di mana arah apotek terdekat?
(Dee mah-nah ah-rah ah-po-tek ter-deh-kaht?)

888. How do I get to the airport from here?
Bagaimana saya menuju bandara dari sini?
(Bah-gah-ee-mah-nah sah-yah meh-noo-joo bahn-da-rah dah-ree see-nee?)

889. Can you point me to the nearest ATM?
Bisa Anda tunjukkan saya ATM terdekat?
(Bee-sah Ahn-dah toon-joohk-kahn sah-yah A-T-M ter-deh-kaht?)

890. I'm lost. Can you help me find my way back to the hotel?
Saya tersesat. Bisakah Anda membantu saya menemukan jalan kembali ke hotel?
(Sah-yah ter-seh-saht. Bee-sah-kah Ahn-dah mehm-bahn-too sah-yah meh-nem-oo-kahn jah-lahn kem-bah-lee keh ho-tel?)

891. Where's the closest gas station?
Di mana stasiun pengisian bahan bakar terdekat?
(Dee mah-nah stah-see-oon peng-ee-see-ahn bah-han bah-kar ter-deh-kaht?)

892. Is there a map of the city available?
Apakah tersedia peta kota?
(Ah-pah-kah ter-seh-dee-ah peh-tah koh-tah?)

893. How far is it to the train station from here?
Seberapa jauh stasiun kereta dari sini?
(Seh-beh-rah-pah jowh stah-see-oon keh-reh-tah dah-ree see-nee?)

894. Which exit should I take to reach the shopping mall?
Pintu keluar mana yang harus saya gunakan untuk mencapai mal?
(Peen-too keh-loo-ar mah-nah yahng hah-roos sah-yah goo-nah-kahn oon-took men-chah-pah-ee mal?)

895. Where can I find a taxi stand around here?
Di mana saya bisa menemukan pangkalan taksi di sekitar sini?
(Dee mah-nah sah-yah bee-sah meh-nem-oo-kahn pahng-kah-lahn tak-see dee seh-kee-tahr see-nee?)

896. Can you direct me to the main tourist attractions?
Bisakah Anda mengarahkan saya ke atraksi wisata utama?
(Bee-sah-kah Ahn-dah meng-ah-rah-kahn sah-yah keh at-rak-see wee-sah-tah oo-tah-mah?)

> **Fun Fact:** Balinese Hinduism is a unique form of Hinduism practiced in Bali.

897. I need to go to the hospital. Can you provide directions?
Saya perlu pergi ke rumah sakit. Bisa Anda memberikan petunjuk?
(Sah-yah per-loo per-gee keh roo-mah sah-keet. Bee-sah Ahn-dah mem-beh-ree-kahn peh-toon-joohk?)

898. Is there a park nearby where I can go for a walk?
Apakah ada taman terdekat di mana saya bisa berjalan-jalan?
(Ah-pah-kah ah-dah tah-man ter-deh-kaht dee mah-nah sah-yah bee-sah behr-jah-lan-jah-lan?)

899. Which street should I take to reach the museum?
Jalan mana yang harus saya ambil untuk mencapai museum?
(Jah-lahn mah-nah yahng hah-roos sah-yah ahm-beel oon-took men-chah-pah-ee moo-seh-oom?)

900. How do I get to the concert venue?
Bagaimana cara saya pergi ke tempat konser?
(Bah-gah-ee-mah-nah kah-rah sah-yah per-gee keh tem-paht kon-ser?)

901. Can you guide me to the nearest public restroom?
Bisa Anda tunjukkan saya ke toilet umum terdekat?
(Bee-sah Ahn-dah toon-joohk-kahn sah-yah keh toh-leet oo-moom ter-deh-kaht?)

902. Where's the best place to catch a cab in this area?
Di mana tempat terbaik untuk mendapatkan taksi di area ini?
(Dee mah-nah tem-paht ter-bah-ik oon-took men-dah-pah-tahn tak-see dee ah-ree-ah ee-nee?)

Buying Tickets

903. I'd like to buy a one-way ticket to downtown, please.
Saya ingin membeli tiket satu arah ke pusat kota, tolong.
(Sah-yah een-geen mem-beh-lee tee-ket sah-too ah-rah keh poo-saht koh-tah, toh-long.)

904. How much is a round-trip ticket to the airport?
Berapa harga tiket pulang-pergi ke bandara?
(Beh-rah-pah hahr-gah tee-ket poo-lahng-per-gee keh bahn-dah-rah?)

905. Do you accept credit cards for ticket purchases?
Apakah Anda menerima kartu kredit untuk pembelian tiket?
(Ah-pah-kah Ahn-dah meh-nair-rah-mah kar-too kreh-deet oon-took pem-beh-lee-ahn tee-ket?)

906. Can I get a student discount on this train ticket?
Apakah saya bisa mendapatkan diskon pelajar untuk tiket kereta ini?
(Ah-pah-kah sah-yah bee-sah men-dah-pah-tahn dees-kon peh-lah-jahr oon-took tee-ket keh-reh-tah ee-nee?)

907. Is there a family pass available for the bus?
Apakah ada pass keluarga untuk bus?
(Ah-pah-kah ah-dah pahs keh-loo-ahr-gah oon-took boos?)

908. What's the fare for a child on the subway?
Berapa tarif anak di kereta bawah tanah?
(Be-rah-pah tah-rif ah-nak dee keh-reh-tah bawah tah-nah?)

909. Are there any senior citizen discounts for tram tickets?
Apakah ada diskon untuk lansia pada tiket tram?
(Ah-pah-kah ah-dah dis-kon oon-took lan-see-ah pah-dah tee-ket tram?)

910. Do I need to make a reservation for the express train?
Apakah saya perlu membuat reservasi untuk kereta ekspres?
(Ah-pah-kah sah-yah per-loo meh-mboo-at re-ser-va-see oon-took keh-reh-tah eks-pres?)

911. Can I upgrade to first class on this flight?
Bisakah saya naik kelas ke kelas pertama pada penerbangan ini?
(Bee-sah-kah sah-yah na-ik keh-las keh keh-las per-tah-mah pah-dah peh-ner-bang-an een-ee?)

912. Are there any extra fees for luggage on this bus?
Apakah ada biaya tambahan untuk bagasi di bus ini?
(Ah-pah-kah ah-dah bee-ah-yah tam-bah-han oon-took bah-gah-see dee boos een-ee?)

913. I'd like to book a sleeper car for the overnight train.
Saya ingin memesan gerbong tidur untuk kereta malam.
(Sah-yah een-geen meh-me-san ger-bong tee-door oon-took keh-reh-tah mah-lam.)

914. What's the schedule for the next ferry to the island?
Bagaimana jadwal kapal feri berikutnya ke pulau?
(Bah-gah-ee-mah-nah jah-dwal kah-pal fe-ree be-ree-koot-nyah keh poo-low?)

915. Are there any available seats on the evening bus to the beach?
Apakah ada kursi tersedia di bus malam ke pantai?
(Ah-pah-kah ah-dah koor-see ter-se-dee-ah dee boos mah-lam keh pahn-tah-ee?)

916. Can I pay for my metro ticket with a mobile app?
Apakah saya bisa membayar tiket metro dengan aplikasi seluler?
(Ah-pah-kah sah-yah bee-sah mem-bah-yar tee-ket meh-tro dehng-an ah-plee-kah-see se-loo-ler?)

917. Is there a discount for purchasing tickets online?
Apakah ada diskon untuk pembelian tiket secara online?
(Ah-pah-kah ah-dah dis-kon oon-took pem-bee-lee-an tee-ket se-kah-rah on-line?)

918. How much is the parking fee at the train station?
Berapa biaya parkir di stasiun kereta?
(Be-rah-pah bee-ah-yah par-keer dee stah-see-oon keh-reh-tah?)

919. I'd like to reserve two seats for the next shuttle bus.
Saya ingin memesan dua kursi untuk bus antar-jemput berikutnya.
(Sah-yah een-geen meh-me-san doo-ah koor-see oon-took boos an-tar-jem-poot be-ree-koot-nyah.)

920. Do I need to validate my ticket before boarding the tram?
Apakah saya perlu memvalidasi tiket saya sebelum naik tram?
(Ah-pah-kah sah-yah per-loo mem-vah-lee-dah-see tee-ket sah-yah se-be-loom na-ik tram?)

921. Can I buy a monthly pass for the subway?
Bisakah saya membeli abonemen bulanan untuk metro?
(Bee-sah-kah sah-yah mem-beh-lee ah-boh-ne-men boo-lah-nan oon-took meh-tro?)

922. Are there any group rates for the boat tour?
Apakah ada tarif grup untuk tur perahu?
(Ah-pah-kah ah-dah tah-rif groop oon-took toor peh-rah-oo?)

Travel Story: In a traditional market in Pontianak, a herbal medicine seller described her remedies as "Seperti emas hijau," or "Like green gold," for their precious and healing nature.

Arranging Travel

923. I need to book a flight to Paris for next week.
Saya perlu memesan penerbangan ke Paris untuk minggu depan.
(Sah-yah per-loo meh-me-san peh-ner-bang-an keh Pa-rees oon-took ming-goo deh-pan.)

924. What's the earliest departure time for the high-speed train?
Apa waktu keberangkatan paling awal untuk kereta api cepat?
(Ah-pah wahk-too keh-beh-rang-kah-tan pah-ling ah-wal oon-took keh-reh-tah ah-pee cheh-pat?)

925. Can I change my bus ticket to a later time?
Bisakah saya mengubah tiket bus saya ke waktu yang lebih belakangan?
(Bee-sah-kah sah-yah meng-ooh-bah tee-ket boos sah-yah keh wahk-too yahng leh-beeh beh-lah-kang-ahn?)

926. I'd like to rent a car for a week.
Saya ingin menyewa mobil selama seminggu.
(Sah-yah een-geen men-ye-wah moh-beel se-lah-mah seh-ming-goo.)

927. Is there a direct flight to New York from here?
Apakah ada penerbangan langsung ke New York dari sini?
(Ah-pah-kah ah-dah peh-ner-bang-an lang-soong keh New York dah-ree see-nee?)

928. I need to cancel my reservation for the cruise.
Saya perlu membatalkan reservasi saya untuk pelayaran.
(Sah-yah per-loo mem-bah-tal-kan re-ser-va-see sah-yah oon-took peh-lay-ah-ran.)

929. Can you help me find a reliable taxi service for airport transfers?
Bisakah Anda membantu saya menemukan layanan taksi yang terpercaya untuk transfer bandara?
(Bee-sah-kah Ahn-dah mem-bahn-too sah-yah meh-nem-oo-kan lay-an-an tak-see yahng ter-per-chah-yah oon-took trans-fer ban-dah-rah?)

930. I'm interested in a guided tour of the city.
How can I arrange that?
Saya tertarik dengan tur berpemandu di kota ini. Bagaimana saya bisa mengaturnya?
(Sah-yah ter-tah-reek dehng-an toor ber-peh-man-doo dee koh-tah een-ee. Bah-gah-ee-mah-nah sah-yah bee-sah meng-ah-toor-nyah?)

931. Do you have any information on overnight buses to the capital?
Apakah Anda memiliki informasi tentang bus malam ke ibu kota?
(Ah-pah-kah Ahn-dah meh-mee-lee een-for-mah-see ten-tang boos mah-lam keh ee-boo koh-tah?)

932. I'd like to purchase a travel insurance policy for my trip.
Saya ingin membeli polis asuransi perjalanan untuk perjalanan saya.
(Sah-yah een-geen mem-beh-lee poh-lees ah-soo-ran-see per-jah-lah-nan oon-took per-jah-lah-nan sah-yah.)

933. Can you recommend a good travel agency for vacation packages?
Bisakah Anda merekomendasikan agen perjalanan yang baik untuk paket liburan?
(Bee-sah-kah Ahn-dah meh-re-koh-men-dah-see-kan ah-gen per-ja-lah-nan yahng bah-ik oon-took pah-ket lee-boo-ran?)

934. I need a seat on the evening ferry to the island.
Saya memerlukan tempat di feri malam menuju pulau itu.
(Sah-yah meh-mehr-loo-kan tem-pat dee feh-ree mah-lahm meh-noo-joo poo-lah-oo ee-too.)

935. How can I check the departure times for international flights?
Bagaimana saya bisa memeriksa waktu keberangkatan untuk penerbangan internasional?
(Bah-gah-ee-mah-nah sah-yah bee-sah meh-meh-reek-sah wah-ktoo keh-beh-rang-kah-tan oon-took peh-ner-bang-an in-ter-nah-see-oh-nal?)

936. Is there a shuttle service from the hotel to the train station?
Apakah ada layanan shuttle dari hotel ke stasiun kereta?
(Ah-pah-kah ah-dah lay-ah-nan shuh-tel dah-ree ho-tel keh stah-see-oon keh-reh-tah?)

937. I'd like to charter a private boat for a day trip.
Saya ingin menyewa kapal pribadi untuk perjalanan sehari.
(Sah-yah een-geen meh-nye-wah kah-pal pree-bah-dee oon-took per-ja-lah-nan seh-hah-ree.)

938. Can you assist me in booking a vacation rental apartment?
Bisakah Anda membantu saya dalam memesan apartemen sewaan liburan?
(Bee-sah-kah Ahn-dah mehm-bahn-too sah-yah dahlam meh-meh-sahn ah-par-teh-men sew-ah-an lee-boo-ran?)

939. I need to arrange transportation for a group of 20 people.
Saya perlu mengatur transportasi untuk kelompok 20 orang.
(Sah-yah per-loo meng-ah-toor trans-por-tah-see oon-took keh-lom-pok doo-ah-pool oh-rang.)

940. What's the best way to get from the airport to the city center?
Apa cara terbaik untuk pergi dari bandara ke pusat kota?
(Ah-pah chah-rah ter-bah-ik oon-took per-ghee dah-ree ban-dah-rah keh poo-sat koh-tah?)

941. Can you help me find a pet-friendly accommodation option?
Bisakah Anda membantu saya menemukan pilihan akomodasi yang ramah hewan peliharaan?
(Bee-sah-kah Ahn-dah mehm-bahn-too sah-yah meh-neh-moo-kan peel-ee-han ah-koh-moh-dah-see yahng rah-mah heh-wahn peh-lee-hah-rahn?)

942. I'd like to plan a road trip itinerary for a scenic drive.
Saya ingin merencanakan itinerary perjalanan darat untuk mengemudi dengan pemandangan yang indah.
(Sah-yah een-geen meh-ren-chah-nah-kan ee-tee-neh-rah-ree per-ja-lah-nan dah-rat oon-took meng-eh-moo-dee dehng-an peh-man-dahng-an yahng een-dah.)

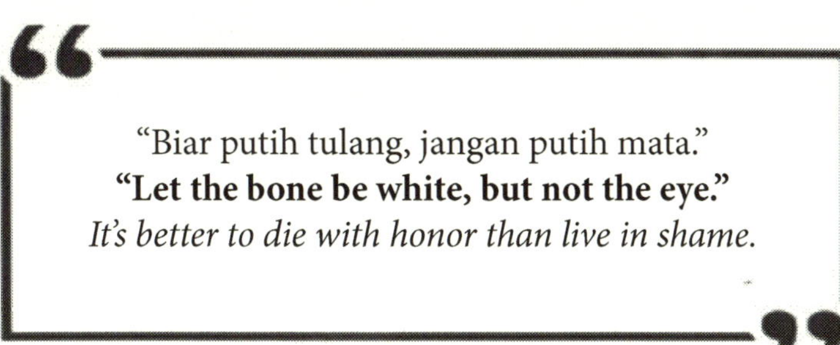
"Biar putih tulang, jangan putih mata."
"Let the bone be white, but not the eye."
It's better to die with honor than live in shame.

Word Search Puzzle: Transport & Directions

CAR
MOBIL
BUS
BUS
AIRPORT
BANDARA
SUBWAY
METRO
TAXI
TAKSI
STREET
JALAN
MAP
PETA
DIRECTION
ARAH
TRAFFIC
LALU LINTAS
PARKING
PARKIR
PEDESTRIAN
PEJALAN KAKI
HIGHWAY
JALAN RAYA
BRIDGE
JEMBATAN
ROUNDABOUT
BUNDARAN
TICKET
TICKET

A R A H X B Q Y S P N Y J Y O
H B D T E Z I T T O A S A L C
V I R G G P R M I W O M L W T
T V G F C E R T B O Q D A W E
Q I F H E U C U W Q F X N B T
A L C T W E S M K A K I M Y I
T C A K R A T G N I K R A P I
E K H I E N Y R N A L A J I T
P S D E D T D M O W Z D H H A
X K L J U P L O R P R H S R R
O Z A D B I K B H I R Y O L A
P R L P N H N I C W K I G X D
C C U T X A C L B T T R A X N
B A A S L M S U S A U J A N A
G S R A I J S C G K O W B P B
J T J E G D I R B S B P Q L A
N E X V D X A N R I A F X L L
P A I N B A A A N T D J B V W
N U T K I R Y C A N N D N Q N
B F C A A A A R I A U Q H S H
P B I D B N O Q R W O Y I S T
P E N B V M K U T M R E S H G
E U Z T W J E Q S T I C K E T
B C S U R E Z J E S W S P F Q
I N M Q J A R K D W M H P S Q
M E T R O T F D E M Z K N D K
N X K N O B A F P M Y I F V U
U G F L T S B X I K V J O V H
P D V S U B N W I C F E A H D
W F O R R I B V C S G S W F T

Correct Answers:

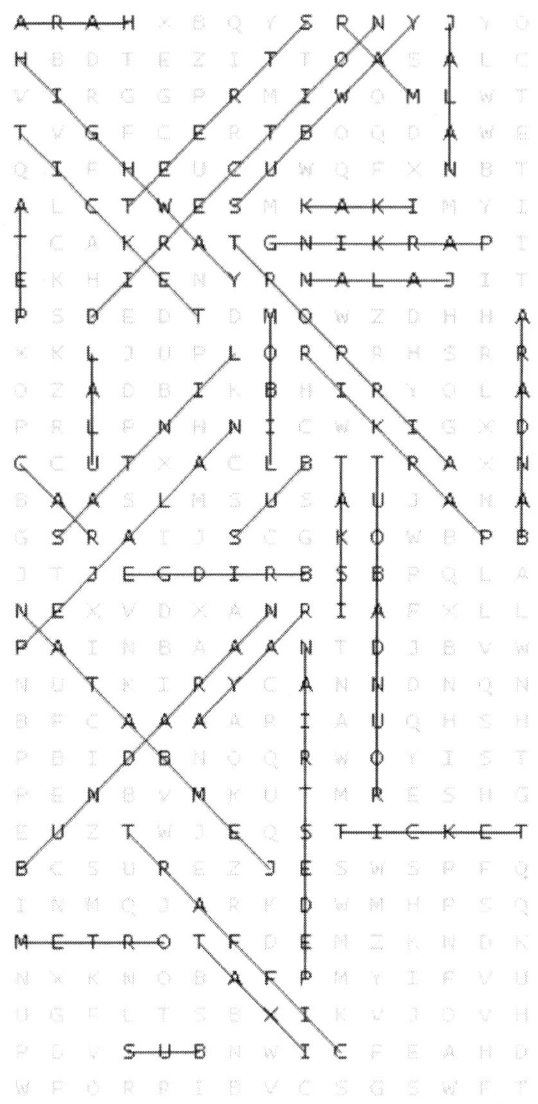

SPECIAL OCCASIONS

- EXPRESSING WELL WISHES AND CONGRATULATIONS -
- CELEBRATIONS AND CULTURAL EVENTS -
- GIVING AND RECEIVING GIFTS -

Expressing Well Wishes & Congratulations

943. Congratulations on your graduation!
Selamat atas kelulusanmu!
(Se-lah-mat ah-tas keh-loo-loo-sahn-moo!)

944. Best wishes for a long and happy marriage.
Semoga pernikahanmu panjang dan bahagia.
(Seh-moh-gah per-nee-kah-han-moo pahn-jahng dahn bah-hah-gee-ah.)

945. Happy anniversary to a wonderful couple.
Selamat ulang tahun untuk pasangan yang luar biasa.
(Se-lah-mat oo-lahng tah-hoon oon-took pah-sahn-gahn yahng loo-ar bee-ah-sah.)

946. Wishing you a speedy recovery.
Semoga cepat sembuh.
(Seh-moh-gah che-paht sem-boo.)

947. Congratulations on your new job!
Selamat atas pekerjaan barumu!
(Se-lah-mat ah-tas pe-ker-ja-an bah-roo-moo!)

> **Travel Story:** In a bustling night market in Makassar, a street food vendor referred to his recipe as "Rahasia turun temurun," meaning "An inherited secret," showcasing the depth of traditional culinary knowledge.

948. May your retirement be filled with joy and relaxation.
Semoga pensiunmu dipenuhi dengan kegembiraan dan relaksasi.
(Seh-moh-gah pen-see-oon-moo dee-peh-noo-hee deh-ngan keh-gem-bee-ra-an dahn re-lak-sah-see.)

949. Best wishes on your engagement.
Selamat atas pertunanganmu.
(Se-lah-mat ah-tas per-too-nahn-gahn-moo.)

950. Happy birthday! Have an amazing day.
Selamat ulang tahun! Semoga harimu menyenangkan.
(Se-lah-mat oo-lahng tah-hoon! Seh-moh-gah hah-ree-moo mehn-yen-ang-kahn.)

> **Cultural Insight:** Once a central part of the global spice trade, Indonesian spices significantly influenced world history.

951. Wishing you success in your new venture.
Semoga sukses di usaha barumu.
(Seh-moh-gah sook-ses dee oo-sah-hah bah-roo-moo.)

952. Congratulations on your promotion!
Selamat atas kenaikan pangkatmu!
(Se-lah-mat ah-tas keh-nah-ee-kahn pahng-kaht-moo!)

953. Good luck on your exam—you've got this!
Semoga berhasil di ujianmu – kamu pasti bisa!
(Seh-moh-gah behr-hah-seel dee oo-jee-ahn-moo – kah-moo pahs-tee bee-sah!)

954. Best wishes for a safe journey.
Semoga perjalananmu aman dan nyaman.
(Seh-moh-gah per-ja-lah-nahn-moo ah-mahn dahn nyah-mahn.)

955. Happy retirement! Enjoy your newfound freedom.
Selamat menikmati pensiun! Nikmati kebebasan barumu.
(Se-lah-mat meh-nee-kmah-tee pen-see-oon! Nee-kmah-tee keh-beh-bah-sahn bah-roo-moo.)

956. Congratulations on your new home.
Selamat atas rumah barumu.
(Se-lah-mat ah-tas roo-mah bah-roo-moo.)

957. Wishing you a lifetime of love and happiness.
Semoga cinta dan kebahagiaan selama hidupmu.
(Seh-moh-gah cheen-tah dahn keh-bah-hah-gee-ahn se-lah-mah hee-doop-moo.)

958. Best wishes on your upcoming wedding.
Semoga pernikahanmu yang akan datang penuh kebahagiaan.
(Seh-moh-gah per-nee-kah-han-moo yahng ah-kahn dah-tahng peh-nooh keh-bah-hah-gee-ahn.)

959. Congratulations on the arrival of your baby.
Selamat atas kelahiran bayimu.
(Se-lah-mat ah-tas keh-lah-hee-rahn bah-yee-moo.)

960. Sending you warmest thoughts and prayers.
Mengirimkanmu pikiran hangat dan doa.
(Meng-ee-reem-kahn-moo pee-kee-rahn hahng-aht dahn doh-ah.)

961. Happy holidays and a joyful New Year!
Selamat hari libur dan Tahun Baru yang ceria!
(Se-lah-mat hah-ree lee-boor dahn Tah-hoon Bah-roo yahng cheh-ree-ah!)

962. Wishing you a wonderful and prosperous future.
Semoga masa depanmu cerah dan sukses.
(Seh-moh-gah mah-sah deh-pahn-moo cheh-rah dahn sook-ses.)

Idiomatic Expression: "Diam-diam menghanyutkan." - Meaning: "Working quietly but effectively." (Literal translation: "Silently drifting away.")

Celebrations & Cultural Events

963. I'm excited to attend the festival this weekend.
Saya sangat bersemangat untuk menghadiri festival akhir pekan ini.
(Sah-yah sahng-aht ber-seh-mahng-aht oon-took meng-hah-dee-ree fes-tee-val ahk-heer peh-kahn ee-nee.)

964. Let's celebrate this special occasion together.
Mari kita rayakan kesempatan spesial ini bersama.
(Mah-ree kee-tah rah-yah-kahn keh-sehm-pah-tahn speh-see-ahl ee-nee ber-sah-mah.)

> **Fun Fact:** Indonesia is one of the world's top coffee producers, famous for Kopi Luwak.

965. The cultural parade was a vibrant and colorful experience.
Pawai budaya itu adalah pengalaman yang penuh warna dan hidup.
(Pah-wah-ee boo-dah-yah ee-too ah-dah-lah peng-ah-lah-mahn yahng peh-nooh wah-rnah dahn hee-doop.)

966. I look forward to the annual family reunion.
Saya menantikan reuni keluarga tahunan.
(Sah-yah meh-nahn-tee-kahn re-oo-nee keh-loo-ahr-gah tah-hoo-nahn.)

967. The fireworks display at the carnival was spectacular.
Pertunjukan kembang api di karnaval itu spektakuler.
(Per-toon-joo-kahn kem-bahng ah-pee dee kar-nah-vahl ee-too spek-tah-koo-ler.)

968. It's always a blast at the neighborhood block party.
Pesta blok di lingkungan selalu menyenangkan.
(Pes-tah blok dee leeng-koon-gahn se-lah-loo men-yen-ang-kahn.)

969. Attending the local cultural fair is a tradition.
Menghadiri pameran budaya lokal adalah tradisi.
(Meng-hah-dee-ree pah-meh-ran boo-dah-yah loh-kahl ah-dah-lah trah-dee-see.)

970. I'm thrilled to be part of the community celebration.
Saya sangat senang menjadi bagian dari perayaan komunitas.
(Sah-yah sahng-aht seh-nang mehn-jah-dee bah-gee-ahn da-ree peh-rah-yahn koh-moo-nee-tahs.)

971. The music and dancing at the wedding were fantastic.
Musik dan tarian di pernikahan itu fantastis.
(Moo-seek dahn tah-ree-ahn dee per-nee-kah-han ee-too fahn-tahs-tees.)

972. Let's join the festivities at the holiday parade.
Mari bergabung dalam perayaan di parade hari libur.
(Mah-ree ber-gah-boong dah-lahm peh-rah-yahn dee pah-rah-deh hah-ree lee-boor.)

973. The cultural exchange event was enlightening.
Acara pertukaran budaya itu sangat pencerahan.
(Ah-chah-rah per-too-kah-rahn boo-dah-yah ee-too sahng-aht pehn-cheh-rah-hahn.)

974. The food at the international festival was delicious.
Makanan di festival internasional itu lezat.
(Mah-kah-nahn dee fes-tee-vahl een-ter-nah-see-oh-nahl ee-too leh-zaht.)

Travel Story: On a scenic drive through the Flores Island, a local driver described the journey as "Berliku-liku bagai ular," literally "Winding like a snake," to express the adventurous nature of the road.

975. I had a great time at the costume party.
Saya sangat menikmati di pesta kostum.
(Sah-yah sahng-aht meh-nee-kmah-tee dee pes-tah kos-toom.)

976. Let's toast to a memorable evening!
Ayo bersulang untuk malam yang tak terlupakan!
(Ah-yo ber-soo-lang oon-took mah-lahm yahng tahk ter-loo-pah-kahn!)

977. The concert was a musical extravaganza.
Konser itu adalah pertunjukan musik yang luar biasa.
(Kohn-ser ee-too ah-dah-lah per-toon-joo-kahn moo-seek yahng loo-ahr bee-ah-sah.)

978. I'm looking forward to the art exhibition.
Saya menantikan pameran seni.
(Sah-yah meh-nahn-tee-kahn pah-meh-rahn seh-nee.)

979. The theater performance was outstanding.
Pertunjukan teater itu sangat luar biasa.
(Per-toon-joo-kahn teh-ah-ter ee-too sahng-aht loo-ahr bee-ah-sah.)

980. We should participate in the charity fundraiser.
Kita harus berpartisipasi dalam penggalangan dana amal.
(Kee-tah hah-roos ber-par-tee-see-pah-see dah-lahm peng-gah-lahng-ahn dah-nah ah-mahl.)

981. The sports tournament was thrilling to watch.
Menonton turnamen olahraga itu sangat mendebarkan.
(Meh-non-ton toor-nah-mehn oh-lah-rah-gah ee-too sahng-aht mehn-deh-bar-kahn.)

982. Let's embrace the local customs and traditions.
Mari kita peluk adat dan tradisi lokal.
(Mah-ree kee-tah peh-look ah-daht dahn trah-dee-see loh-kahl.)

Giving and Receiving Gifts

983. I hope you like this gift I got for you.
Saya harap kamu menyukai hadiah ini yang saya belikan untukmu.
(Sah-yah hah-rap kah-moo meh-nyoo-kah-ee hah-dee-ah een-ee yahng sah-yah beh-lee-kahn oon-took-moo.)

984. Thank you for the thoughtful present!
Terima kasih atas hadiah yang penuh perhatian ini!
(Teh-ree-mah kah-seeh ah-tahs hah-dee-ah yahng peh-nooh pehr-hah-tee-ahn een-ee!)

985. It's a token of my appreciation.
Ini adalah tanda penghargaan saya.
(Ee-nee ah-dah-lah tahn-dah pehng-har-gah-ahn sah-yah.)

986. Here's a little something to brighten your day.
Ini sedikit sesuatu untuk mencerahkan harimu.
(Ee-nee seh-dee-keet seh-soo-ah-too oon-took mehn-cheh-rah-kahn hah-ree-moo.)

987. I brought you a souvenir from my trip.
Saya membawakanmu suvenir dari perjalanan saya.
(Sah-yah mehm-bah-wah-kahn-moo soo-veh-neer dah-ree pehr-jah-lah-nahn sah-yah.)

988. This gift is for you on your special day.
Hadiah ini untukmu di hari spesialmu.
(Hah-dee-ah een-ee oon-took-moo dee hah-ree speh-see-ahl-moo.)

989. I got this with you in mind.
Saya mendapatkan ini dengan memikirkanmu.
(Sah-yah mehn-dah-pah-tahn een-ee dehng-an meh-mee-keer-kahn-moo.)

990. You shouldn't have, but I love it!
Kamu tidak perlu, tapi saya sangat menyukainya!
(Kah-moo tee-dahk pehr-loo, tah-pee sah-yah sahng-aht meh-nyoo-kah-ee-nyah!)

991. It's a small gesture of my gratitude.
Ini adalah gestur kecil dari rasa terima kasih saya.
(Ee-nee ah-dah-lah ges-toor keh-cheel dah-ree rah-sah teh-ree-mah kah-seeh sah-yah.)

992. I wanted to give you a little surprise.
Saya ingin memberimu kejutan kecil.
(Sah-yah een-geen mehm-behr-ee-moo keh-joo-tahn keh-cheel.)

993. I hope this gift brings you joy.
Saya harap hadiah ini membawa kebahagiaan untukmu.
(Sah-yah hah-rap hah-dee-ah een-ee mehm-bah-wah keh-bah-hah-gee-ahn oon-took-moo.)

994. It's a symbol of our friendship.
Ini adalah simbol dari persahabatan kita.
(Ee-nee ah-dah-lah seem-bol dah-ree pehr-sah-hah-bah-tahn kee-tah.)

995. This is just a token of my love.
Ini hanya tanda dari cinta saya.
(Ee-nee hahn-yah tahn-dah dah-ree cheen-tah sah-yah.)

996. I knew you'd appreciate this.
Saya tahu kamu akan menghargai ini.
(Sah-yah tah-hoo kah-moo ah-kahn mehng-har-gah-ee een-ee.)

997. I wanted to spoil you a bit.
Saya ingin memanjakanmu sedikit.
(Sah-yah een-geen mehm-pahn-jah-kahn-moo seh-dee-keet.)

998. This gift is for your hard work.
Hadiah ini untuk kerja kerasmu.
(Hah-dee-ah ee-nee oon-took kehr-jah keh-ras-moo.)

999. I hope you find this useful.
Semoga kamu menemukan ini berguna.
(Seh-moh-gah kah-moo meh-ne-moo-kahn ee-nee behr-goo-nah.)

1000. It's a sign of my affection.
Ini adalah tanda kasih sayang saya.
(Ee-nee ah-dah-lah tahn-dah kah-seeh sah-yahng sah-yah.)

1001. I brought you a little memento.
Saya membawakanmu kenang-kenangan kecil.
(*Sah-yah mehm-bah-wah-kahn-moo keh-nahng-keh-nahng-an keh-cheel.)*

"Tak lapuk dek hujan, tak lekang dek panas."
"Neither decayed by rain nor faded by the sun."
Something that endures all challenges or the test of time.

Interactive Challenge: Special Occasions

(Link each English word with their corresponding meaning in Indonesian)

1) Celebration	Kejutan
2) Gift	Liburan
3) Party	Pesta
4) Anniversary	Perayaan
5) Congratulations	Pernikahan
6) Wedding	Selamat
7) Birthday	Salam
8) Graduation	Wisuda
9) Holiday	Hadiah
10) Ceremony	Hari ulang tahun
11) Tradition	Tradisi
12) Festive	Upacara
13) Greeting	Ulang tahun
14) Toast	Bersulang
15) Surprise	Meriah

Correct Answers:

1. Celebration - Perayaan
2. Gift - Hadiah
3. Party - Pesta
4. Anniversary - Ulang tahun
5. Congratulations - Selamat
6. Wedding - Pernikahan
7. Birthday - Hari ulang tahun
8. Graduation - Wisuda
9. Holiday - Liburan
10. Ceremony - Upacara
11. Tradition - Tradisi
12. Festive - Meriah
13. Greeting - Salam
14. Toast - Bersulang
15. Surprise - Kejutan

CONCLUSION

Congratulations on reaching the final chapter of "The Ultimate Indonesian Phrasebook." As you embark on your journey to explore the diverse and rich culture of Indonesia, from the magnificent temples of Bali to the bustling streets of Jakarta, your dedication to mastering Indonesian is commendable.

This phrasebook has been your companion, providing you with key phrases and expressions to seamlessly enhance your communication. You've progressed from basic greetings like "Halo" and "Selamat sore" to more complex expressions, preparing you for a range of interactions, immersive experiences, and a deeper appreciation of Indonesia's unique heritage.

Embracing the challenge of language proficiency is an enriching pursuit. Your commitment has established a solid foundation for fluency in Indonesian. Remember, language is not merely a communication tool; it's a bridge to understanding a culture's heart and soul.

If this phrasebook has contributed to your language learning journey, I'd be thrilled to hear about it! Connect with me on Instagram: **@adriangruszka**. Share your stories, seek advice, or simply drop a "Halo!" I'd be overjoyed if you mention this book on social media and tag me – I look forward to celebrating your progress in mastering Indonesian.

For more resources, detailed insights, and updates, please visit **www.adriangee.com**. There, you'll discover abundant information, including recommended courses and a community of language enthusiasts ready to support your ongoing learning adventure.

Learning a new language opens doors to fresh relationships and perspectives. Your passion for learning and adapting is your key strength on this linguistic journey. Embrace every chance to learn, interact, and deepen your understanding of Indonesian culture and life.

Selamat berjuang! (Good luck!) Continue to practice diligently, hone your skills, and most importantly, enjoy every moment of your Indonesian language adventure.

Terima kasih banyak! (Thank you very much!) for choosing this phrasebook. May your future explorations be enriched with meaningful dialogues and achievements as you delve deeper into the captivating world of languages!

- Adrian Gee

Made in the USA
Columbia, SC
12 June 2025

59356191R00145